Speedball.

24th EDITION

100 YEARS

A Comprehensive Guide to Pen & Brush Lettering

Originated by Ross F. George

Angela Vangalis • Randall M. Hasson
Editors

CONTRIBUTING ARTISTS

Georgia Angelopoulos
Yukimi Annand
Luca Barcellona
Dick Beasley
Jill Bell
Gemma Black
Charles Borges de Oliveira
Larry Brady
Marsha Brady
John Burns
Fr. Edward Catich
Barbara Calzolari

Karen Charatan
Michael Clark
Barbara Close
Harvest Crittenden
Nick Curtis
Rick Cusick
Judy Detrick
John Downer
Inga Dubay
Carol DuBosch
Ward Dunham
Lisa Engelbrecht

Reggie Ezell
Joanne Fink
Marian Gault
Risa Gettler
Barbara Getty
Julie Gray
Georgianna Greenwood
Sharon Hanse
Randall Hasson
Heather Held
Paul Herrera
Eliza A. Holliday

Cynthia Hollandsworth
Erwin Indrawan
Martin Jackson
Judy Kastin
Mike Kecseg
Todd Klein
Louie Lemoine
Yves Leterme
Jeff Levine
Katherine Malmsten
Cliff Mansley
Don Marsh

Kathy Milici
Holly Monroe
Barry Morentz
Vivian Mungall
Mark Oatis
Amity Parks
Izzy Pludwinski
Marilyn Reaves
Carl Rohrs
CC Sadler
Robert Saslow
Linda Schnieder

Tom Seibert
Debi Sementelli
Robert Slimbach
John Stevens
John Studden
Michael Sull
Janet Takahashi
Leslie Tardy
Peter Thornton
Mark Van Stone
Angela Vangalis
Julian Waters

Sheila Waters
Noel Weber
Jake Weidmann
Eleanor Winters
Jim Woodring
Lilli Wronker
Sharon Zeugin

Speedball Textbook: 24th Edition
A Comprehensive Guide to Pen & Brush Lettering

Art Direction, Research & Production
Angela Vangalis, Randall M. Hasson

Cover, Design & Layout
Angela Vangalis

Inside Cover: Monograms and art produced by William Hugh Gordon, Ross F. George and their staff artists.

Illustrations: Ross F. George, Janet Takahashi

Published by:
Speedball Art Products Company
2301 Speedball Road, Statesville, NC 28677

ISBN 978-0-9906065-4-3

For more information please visit
www.speedballart.com

ACKNOWLEDGEMENTS

This Centennial Edition commemorates the lettering instruction and inspiration that William Hugh Gordon and Ross F. George created to introduce the newly invented Speedball pen in 1915. As one of the many resources on lettering produced since the early 1900s, The Speedball Textbook is unique in its prominence, distribution and popularity; artists in many diverse fields routinely credit it as their "first lettering book."

The alphabets presented in this edition represent some of the finest examples published in the 100 years of The Textbook. The 24th Edition also features new material and instructional sections that represent contemporary lettering styles. As editors, we have had the honor and privilege of working with the Speedball team and the many contributing artists who took the time and effort to help make this edition possible. We extend our heartfelt gratitude to each and every one of them.

Special thanks to Sue George Yourkowski, granddaughter of Ross F. George, who kindly allowed George's archives to be viewed and used for much of the background reference material and content that are reproduced in this volume.

Angela Vangalis

Randall M. Hasson

Title Lettering:

"Sho Card Gothic" style alphabet by Ross F. George was the inspiration for the title lettering. His illustrated ductus teaches how to make this style of lettering with a brush. *The Speedball Textbook, 12th Edition (1933).*

Speedball Sticks were drawn with a B-Series nib and first appeared in The Speedball Textbook, 11th Edition (1929). Stick figure drawings appear throughout this edition.

TABLE OF CONTENTS

3

1910　1912　1913

4

Circa 1910–1912

Original concept for Speedball nib with a reservoir developed by William H. Gordon and Ross F. George.
This nib was developed to replicate the German expressionist styles of lettering – shown below.

1912

Gordon and George sold two original alphabets and two handmade pens for one dollar. This gave them enough money to make the first 1,000 pen nibs.

Speedball refers to the *speed* of the pen. Nicknamed "Speedball" due to the efficiency it provided lettering artists. This new pen was able to "cut working time in half."

1913

Unnamed pen manufacturer found. Project shelved and contract canceled by Gordon and George.

1913
Patents filed by Gordon & George

1913
Contract with Hunt Pen Company, Camden, New Jersey

Ross F. George at his Seattle shop, 1914.

1915	**1916**	**1918**	**1920**
FIRST EDITION	2ND EDITION	4TH EDITION	5TH EDITION

5

1915
Presenting the Speedball Pen
Gordon & George
The Speedball Textbook began with this 40 page booklet which sold for 50¢. Gordon, George and staff artists identified their published work with monogrammed art.

1916
Modern Pen Lettering–2nd Ed.
Gordon & George

Introduced alphabet construction examples with ductus arrows and notes on letter construction.

1917
Modern Pen Lettering–3rd Ed.
Gordon & George

1918
Modern Pen Lettering–4th Ed.
Gordon & George
Introduced the C-Series nib.
Lettering for Commercial Purposes published by Signs of the Times.

1919
Terminally ill, William Gordon sold his share of Speedball copyrights to Ross F. George.

1920
Modern Pen Lettering–5th Ed.
Ross F. George

1920
Death of William Hugh Gordon, August 23rd.

6

1921	1922	1925	1926
6TH EDITION	**7TH EDITION**	**8TH EDITION**	**9TH EDITION**

1921
Modern Pen Lettering–6th Ed.
Ross F. George
Introduced *Draftsmen & Architects Styles* and border patterns by William Hugh Gordon.

1922
Modern Pen Lettering–7th Ed.
Ross F. George
Introduced new alphabets *Western Letters, Roundhand Script* and *Old English*.

1925
Modern Pen Lettering–8th Ed.
Ross F. George
Expanded *Roundhand Script* to include ductus arrows and practice pages.

1926
Modern Pen Lettering–9th Ed.
Ross F. George
First mention of D-Series pen in *Metropolitan Poster* alphabet.

THE TEXTBOOK THROUGH TIME

1960 — 18TH EDITION

1960
Speedball Textbook: For Pen & Brush Lettering–18th Ed.
by Hunt Pen Co.

This was the last issue Ross F. George worked on and the last 6" x 9" edition size. Introduced the *Steel Brush* and *Chancery Cursive* alphabets.

STEEL BRUSH
Chancery Cursive

1965 — 19TH EDITION

1965
Speedball Textbook: For Pen & Brush Lettering–19th Ed.
"Originated by Ross F. George"
Raymond DaBoll, Sister M. Jeannine, Ralph Loomis, Edgar Moore Contributors.

New smaller 8.5" x 5.5" size. New alphabets included *Humanist, Carolingian, Uncial, Manuscript* and *Blackletter* along with *Celtic* forms. Featured calligraphic broadsides and certificates.

CELTIC

1972 — 20TH EDITION

1972
Speedball Textbook: For Pen & Brush Lettering–20th Ed.
Charles Stoner and Henry Frankenfeld

Early to mid-1970's
Donald Jackson (Scribe to the Queen of England) encouraged calligraphy guild formation. Calligraphic movement began to gain popularity in America.

1985 — 21ST EDITION

1985
Speedball Textbook: The Only Complete Guide to Lettering & Calligraphy–21st Ed.
Charles Stoner and Henry Frankenfeld
Illustrations of pen nibs featuring calligraphy styles.
Introduced a gallery of envelopes and debut of noted calligraphers in many sections of book.

| 1941 | 1948 | 1952 | 1956 |

14TH EDITION | **15TH EDITION** | **16TH EDITION** | **17TH EDITION**

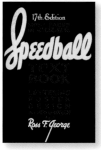

1941
Speedball Textbook: Lettering Poster Design–14th Ed.
Ross F. George

Advertising Moods and *Postrie Caps* lettering appeared.

The adaptation of Lettering to
ADVERTISING MOODS
POSTRIE CAPS

1948
Speedball Textbook: Lettering, Poster Design For Pen & Brush–15th Ed.
Ross F. George

Introduced Flicker Pens with hinged reservoirs.
New alphabets *Speed 'D' Italics*, *D' Speedball Rope*, and *Line Gothic* added along with section on decorated initials.

D' Speedball Rope

1952
Speedball Textbook: Lettering, Poster Design For Pen & Brush–16th Ed.
Ross F. George

Addition of *Free Roman* alphabet and first use of full-color images.

free Roman

1956
Speedball Textbook: Lettering, Poster Design For Pen & Brush–17th Ed.
Ross F. George

Featured revised decorative initials.

1959 – Death of Ross F. George
February 19th

THE TEXTBOOK THROUGH TIME

1927
10TH EDITION

1929
11TH EDITION

1933
12TH EDITION

1938
13TH EDITION

1927

Modern Pen Lettering–10th Ed.

Ross F. George

First full-page announcement of the D-Series pen in *Snappy Styles* with Style D.

1929

*Title changes to **The Speedball Textbook: Modern Pen Lettering**–11th Ed.*

Ross F. George

Speedball inks in assorted colors debuted and were featured on back cover. Introduced *Stunt Roman* alphabet.

1933

Speedball Textbook: Modern Lettering for Pen and Brush–12th Ed.

Ross F. George

Last landscape format edition. Introduced *Built Up Romans* using D-Series nib. *Speedball Sticks* appear.

Speedball Sticks

1938

Modern Lettering for Pen and Brush - Poster Design - Speedball Textbook–13 Ed.

Ross F. George

New vertical format. Introduced *Flat Brush* alphabets with detailed stroke instruction *ShoCard* and *Spurred Gothic* alphabets.

THE TEXTBOOK THROUGH TIME

1991

22ND EDITION

1991
The Speedball Textbook: A Complete Guide to Pen and Brush Lettering–22nd Ed.
Joanne Fink and Judy Kastin

Many full-color images. Introduced *Pointed Brush Lettering* along with *Versals, Neuland* and *Flat Brush* with array of contemporary artists. Also featured invitations, envelope and logo examples.

1999

23RD EDITION

1999
The Speedball Textbook: A Complete Guide to Pen and Brush Lettering–23rd Ed.
Joanne Fink and Judy Kastin

Featured over 100 calligraphers and printed in two-color and full-color format. Introduced *Pointed Pen Variations* and expanded sections on *Calligraphic Terms, Logos* and *Layout & Design.*

pen variations

2015

24TH EDITION

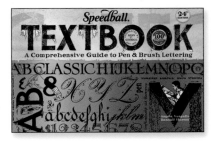

2015
Speedball Textbook: A Complete Guide to Pen & Brush Lettering–24th Ed.
Angela Vangalis and Randall Hasson

This edition commemorates 100 years of the Textbook's publication with newly discovered history of Ross F. George and William Hugh Gordon. Introduces *American Cursive, Bone, Fraktur, Greek* and *Spencerian Script* alphabets with expanded pressurized lettering techniques. New sections on *Comics, Sign Painters, Chalkboard Lettering* and *Lettering for Fonts.*

BoneAlphabet

Basic tools and techniques are the same whether you are lettering for fun or for commercial purposes.

DIP PENS

There are two different kinds of nibs. Both broad-edged and pointed can be inserted into Speedball® pen holders.

Broad-edged nib holder

Classic holder with pointed nib

Oblique holder

Crow Quill nib & holder

When lettering broad-edged hands (e.g. *Italic, Roman, Blackletter*, etc.), select a broad-edged tool like the A-Series, B-Series or C-Series Speedball nibs (available in six sizes). When lettering pointed pen hands, use a flexible pointed nib, like Hunt® No. 99 or No. 103 flexible pointed nibs.

For monoline lettering, select a Speedball A-Series or B-Series nib.

The Crow Quill nib is used for fine lines, drawing and touching up letterforms.

INKS & PAINTS & MARKERS

Water-soluble and waterproof inks are manufactured in a wide array of colors. When using a dip pen, try Speedball's *Super Black India* inks.

Many lettering artists like to control the denseness of the writing fluid by grinding their own *stick ink.*

For color work, transparent watercolor or *gouache* (opaque watercolor) is a preferred medium or try Speedball's *Super Pigmented Acrylic Ink* for rich vivid colors that are archival, waterproof and permanent.

Permanent and water-soluble markers are available for lettering and layout sketches.

CARING FOR NIBS & INKS

* Ink will not flow freely from a dirty pen. Keep pens clean for clean-cut lettering.

* Place a jar of water and a rag or lint-free paper towel nearby for maintaining clean and dry pens.

The Speedball Textbook, 16th Edition (1952).

* The best way to remove dried inks is to scrub them gently with a toothbrush and Speedball Pen Cleaner.

* Organize clean, dry nibs in a small divided container.

* Filling a fountain pen with waterproof or India ink will cause the pen to clog easily.

* Secure an ink bottle to the table with tape to prevent it from accidental spillage.

11

FOUNTAIN PENS

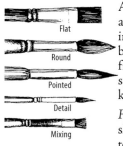

Speedball® Fountain Pens have ink cartridges which automatically feed ink to the nib. The fountain pen nibs are available in Fine (1.1mm), Medium (1.5mm) and Broad (1.9mm) and the ink colors available for the cartridges are Black, Blue, Red, Purple, Green, and Pink.

BRUSHES

Flat

Round

Pointed

Detail

Mixing

Available in pointed and flat shapes and in a variety of sizes, brushes are made from animal hair or synthetic materials, known as *filament*.

Flat brushes with short hair are easiest to control for lettering.

Pointed brushes for lettering should spring back to retain a fine point.

Good quality sable brushes are the most costly and durable. *Short bristle* brushes are used for mixing paint.

PAPER

The type of paper selected is crucial to good lettering, therefore it is important to choose a paper that will work well with the pen and ink. Layout bond is an excellent, economical choice for practice and reproduction work.

For finished pieces, try smooth or vellum surface bristol board or any good quality machine or handmade paper.

Always test the paper with the pen and ink to be used, before doing any project.

Suggested papers include the Bienfang® series:

Graphics 360 Marker & Gridded Paper - excellent choices for practice and when working for reproduction and planning layouts.

Tracing Paper - for tracing and practicing letterforms and developing layout ideas.

#206 Calligraphy Practice Paper - pre-lined, suitable for Series C-2 nibs and pointed pen practice.

#207 Calligraphy Parchment Paper - heavier stock for bookmarks and place cards.

Bristol Board - smooth or vellum surface for lettering to be scanned or for original art.

Arnhem 1618™ - 100% rag, acid-free with a semi-smooth, vellum surface for original artwork.

SETTING UP

+ Establish a place to letter. This area should contain enough space to write comfortably with tools, *pen wipe* and ink within easy reach.

+ Good lighting is essential. The light should be placed on the left side for right-handers to prevent shadows on the working surface and opposite for left-handers.

+ Desk or Table - many lettering artists prefer an adjustable, slanted drawing board that sits on a table, while others arc comfortable working on a flat surface.

+ Choose a comfortable chair to ensure good posture - sitting upright with feet flat to the floor. If standing is preferred, the table should reach the hips.

Cover Sheet

TEXTBOOK

PREPARING TO WRITE WITH A DIP PEN

When using a new metal nib, dip the nib into a small amount of liquid *Gum Arabic* and wipe with a soft rag to remove any oils from the manufacturing process. *Gum Arabic* helps the ink stay in the reservoir for a smoother writing experience.

Place the nib so it is firmly seated within the pen holder using a pen wipe.

LOADING A PEN

Dip the pen nib half-way up the reservoir.

Dip pointed pen nib to the nib's keyhole.

When using gouache or watercolor, mix the desired color in a palette with a mixing brush. Use the mixing brush to load the pen by brushing the paint onto the nib. Shake the pen once to remove excess paint and to avoid blobs from overloading.

13

"How to hold a Speedball pen. Don't lean on the pen. Use free arm movements." The Speedball Textbook, 2nd Edition (1916).

HOW TO HOLD A PEN

Hold the broad-edged pen just like a pencil. Most of the movement comes from the shoulder. The diagram above demonstrates the three points of contact for a right-handed artist. See page 19 for left-handed recommendations.

The pen hold should be comfortable with an even, constant pressure. Keep the writing tip in full contact with the paper when making strokes.

Too much pressure will fatigue the hand very quickly while yielding a distorted width of the nib. Uneven pressure will yield ragged, uneven edges.

ADDITIONAL EQUIPMENT

+ Pencils (3H or 4H for drawing lines)
+ Pencil sharpener
+ Eye dropper for transferring ink
+ Small shallow dish or palette
+ Pen wipe (a small piece of chamois leather) or rag for cleaning nibs
+ Tape (both removable and artist's tape)
+ Eraser (vinyl or kneaded)
+ Water jar for cleaning brushes and nibs
+ T-square
+ Triangle
+ Metal ruler with non-slip cork backing for measuring and drawing lines.
+ Light table or light pad (optional)

BROAD-EDGED PRACTICE

Practice pen control by making repetitive strokes or patterns with an Elegant Writer 3.0mm marker or C-Series (C-2) and Bienfang Gridded paper to measure and monitor the line quality. Start by making squares in 1 square on the grid paper, and lines 5 squares high.

Hold the pen at 0° and draw squares and vertical lines of equal lengths.

Hold the pen at 90° and draw horizontal lines of equal lengths.

+ + +

Draw a combination of both horizontal and verticcal lines of equal lengths.

/////////

Hold the pen at 45° and draw short picket lines 2 or 3 squares tall on the gridded paper. Then draw longer pickets 5 squares in length to pierce the top and bottom lines slightly, as shown.

Become comfortable with making firm, consistent marks and maintaining pen's edge contact on the paper.

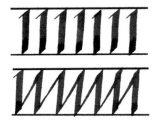

Keep pen at 45° to draw zig zag lines five squares high.

Make arched strokes by holding the pen at 45° to get a ribbon-like thin and thick lines while keeping the edge of the nib on the paper the entire stroke.

HELPFUL HINTS

- When learning, practice larger to analyze and correct letterforms.
- Use a *pen wipe* to aid in fitting a nib into a pen holder without damaging the nib while protecting the fingers from sharp pointed nibs.
- Enlarge the exemplars in this book, trace with a marker or pen and practice the letterforms.
- Write *pangrams* (sentences with every letter of the alphabet) to practice form and establish a rhythm.
- Use a cover sheet to protect good lettering paper from the natural oils in your hand. A cover sheet is simply a piece of layout paper folded in half. Alternatively, a cotton fingerless glove can be used.

𝕿𝖍𝖊 𝖖𝖚𝖎𝖈𝖐 𝖇𝖗𝖔𝖜𝖓 𝖋𝖔𝖝 𝖏𝖚𝖒𝖕𝖘 𝖔𝖛𝖊𝖗 𝖙𝖍𝖊 𝖑𝖆𝖟𝖞 𝖉𝖔𝖌 ·

Panagram in Blackletter, Ward Dunham

The broad-edged nib has a rigid, flat edge that produces thick and thin ribbon-like strokes.

Most broad-edged exemplars, or "hands" in this textbook are illustrated with *ductus* (directional arrows) along with three main elements: the *x-height*, *pen angle* and *weight*.

The letter height or *x-height* establishes the proportion of the body height of the alphabet style.

For example, the *Italic* alphabet is based on an x-height of 5 nib widths with a pen angle of 30° to 40°.

The nib widths are stacked one upon the other starting on the *writing line* (also called the *base line*) and continuing to the *waist line* to form the x-height. The x-height is then repeated to form the as-

cender and *descender* lines, with the *capital line* traditionally two nib widths above the waist line (see diagram below).

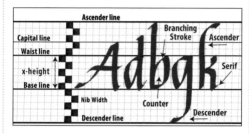

Changing the x-height alters the thickness of the letterform. The example below illustrates the x-height for the word "italic" at four and ten nib widths using the same nib size.

PEN ANGLE

The *pen angle* is made by keeping the nib edge to the base line and determines the characteristic of the alphabet style.

Maintaining the correct angle of the pen nib in relationship to the base line is crucial to any style of lettering.

The pen angle should not be confused with the slant of the letter or cant of the paper.

SLANT LINE & BRANCHING

The *slant line* is a guideline for the slope at which the lettering is written and must remain consistent.

These guides, when placed beneath lettering paper and used with a light table, are very helpful.

The slant, branching and width of the nib, will dictate the *weight* (or thickness) of the letterform.

The *branching* technique of any lettering will dictate the overall slant.

Branching occurs when an arch-shaped stroke connects to the down stroke of a letter. See following page.

15

BRANCHING PRINCIPLES

A way to vary the look of any style of lettering is by analyzing where the points of tangency and/or intersection are in the *branching* of a letter.

Points of Tangency - where the curve of the branch touches the vertical line in relationship to the letter.

Points of Intersection - where the curve of the branch crosses or lies on the vertical line.

The example to the right demonstrates that there are essentially six ways to create a letter style. When used consistently in an alphabet, no one approach is right or wrong.

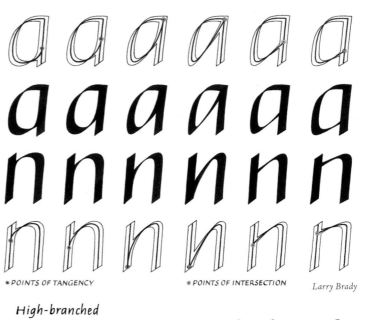

* POINTS OF TANGENCY   * POINTS OF INTERSECTION   *Larry Brady*

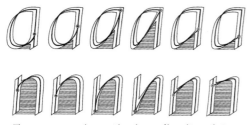

The counter spaces change with each type of branching technique.

5 nib widths

High-branched

Upright, high-branched and formal 30°

4½ Slanted, high-branched and rounded 25°

3½ Slanted, rounded and wide 20°

Sheila Waters

Medium-branched

4½ △ 45° Upright, medium-branched, narrow

5 △ 35° Slanted, medium-branched, narrow

3½ △ 30° Slanted, med.-branched, wide

Low-branched

5 △ 50° Upright, narrow, sharp and icy cold

4½ △ 40° Slanted, low-branched, sharp, windy

3½ △ 30° Slanted, wide and sharp writing

12 △ 35° Tall narrow, light and delicate

2½ △ 25° **Short, wider, heavy and dark**

Sheila Waters

SLANT, WIDTH & ARCH VARIABLES

Each of the preceding examples demonstrates the three main types of branching at three different pen angles, x-heights and slants.

High branching occurs when the arch branches towards the top of the stem. This method is sometimes considered "formal."

Medium branching occurs when the arch branches away from the stem half-way and upward into the second stem.

Low branching occurs when the arch branches away from the stem at its base. This type of branching characterizes an informal style.

These examples explore structure, not personal style. Style grows from structure.

OPTICAL
SPACING
MECHANICAL
SPACING

Note the improvement in legibility effected by the optically equalized spacing above.

Simplified spacing guide for different letters.

IDOKLC

Fit the letters of a word together according to their shape with the area between them pleasingly balanced and you will have units that lend themselves to a good layout. The Speedball Textbook, 13th Edition (1938).

LETTER SPACING

Letters should be fitted so that they will read clearly and give a pleasing effect of evenness throughout each word and sentence.

It is important to note that no two alphabets are spaced in exactly the same manner. Factors like size, style and reading requirements combine to make each word's spacing different.

To account for this variation, Ross F. George created a diagram titled, *Correct Letter Spacing* (shown left), to help lettering artists understand how to space letters correctly and in a "pleasingly uniform" fashion.

GENERAL RULE FOR OPTICAL SPACING

1. There is more space between two straight lines.

2. There is less space between a straight stroke and a curved stroke.

3. The least amount of space is between two round strokes.

LEFT-HANDED WRITERS
and the Broad-Edged Pen

While right-handed artists may position their paper directly in front of them or canted slightly to the right, the left-handed letterer has the unique challenge of determining the most comfortable paper position specific to their lettering style and tools.

The cant of the paper may be adjusted. The recommended approaches for altering the cant of the paper are outlined in the diagram provided on the right.

When referencing the exemplars throughout this textbook, it is important to note that all the ductus indicators are for a right-handed scribe.

As long as the thick and thin strokes are made where they need to be, a "lefty" can choose the most comfortable position for their lettering style.

Options: Try writing upside-down or switch to writing with the right hand. "Lefties" are more ambidextrous than those who are right-handed.

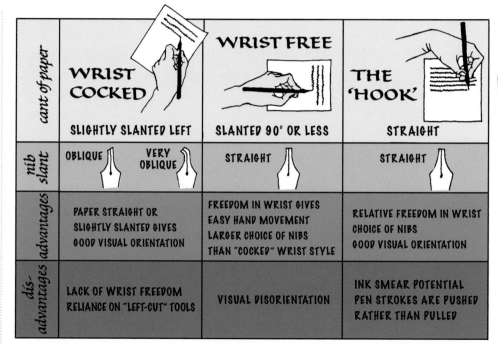

cant of paper	WRIST COCKED	WRIST FREE	THE 'HOOK'
	SLIGHTLY SLANTED LEFT	SLANTED 90° OR LESS	STRAIGHT
nib slant	OBLIQUE VERY OBLIQUE	STRAIGHT	STRAIGHT
advantages	PAPER STRAIGHT OR SLIGHTLY SLANTED GIVES GOOD VISUAL ORIENTATION	FREEDOM IN WRIST GIVES EASY HAND MOVEMENT LARGER CHOICE OF NIBS THAN "COCKED" WRIST STYLE	RELATIVE FREEDOM IN WRIST CHOICE OF NIBS GOOD VISUAL ORIENTATION
dis-advantages	LACK OF WRIST FREEDOM RELIANCE ON "LEFT-CUT" TOOLS	VISUAL DISORIENTATION	INK SMEAR POTENTIAL PEN STROKES ARE PUSHED RATHER THAN PULLED

Georgianna Greenwood

A-SERIES · SQUARE

Patented in 1913 and introduced two years later, the A-Series nib is where it all started for Speedball. The influence of the German styles of lettering required artists to produce work lines of uniform-width, a necessity that proved difficult and tedious when working in smaller sizes. William H. Gordon and Ross F. George set out to find a solution to this ongoing problem, and developed a nib that possessed a square tip, bent to form a "shoe."

This construction allowed artists to create a uniform line with a single stroke, improving efficiencies up to "five times that of traditional methods of the day."

Lettering styles that are suitable for the A-Series nib are any *Gothic* or *Monoline* styles that have lines of uniform width with a squared finish – see opposite page and *Neuland* on page 65.

The A-Series nib can be used in three basic ways to achieve a wide variety of lettering. First, it can be held perpendicular to the base line, keeping the "shoe" of the pen nib flat on the surface – this produces a uniform stroke in any direction with squared beginnings and endings.

Second, it can be held at an angle to achieve either a diamond-shaped beginning and ending or a square finish on a diagonal stroke.

Elementary Principles

abcdefghijklmno
pqrstuvwxyz & nn

Practice using "Elementary Principles" to get familiar with this unique A-Series nib. Presenting the Speedball Pen, 1st Edition (1915).

abcdefghijklmnopqr

Diamond-shaped finishing stroke

Third, it can be turned over on its back to utilize the broad, flat end of the pen to produce either lettering with thicks and thins or to create the serifs on lettering of uniform width as shown adjacent.

A-Series Speedball pen, No. 1. Lettered in less than three minutes. William Hugh Gordon.
The Speedball Textbook, 2nd Edition (1916)

A-Series nib, Michael Clark

"Ragged Rugged" letters made with slight wiggly strokes using an A-Series Speedball nib, by William Hugh Gordon. The Speedball Textbook, 2nd Edition (1916)

STYLE B - ROUND

The B-Series nib was fashioned shortly after the original square style nib, and made its debut in the 2nd Edition of the Textbook, published in 1916.

Like the A-Series, the B-Series has a bent end to form a "shoe" to produce a uniform width line. Unlike its counterpart, the B-Style has a rounded finish, ideal for creating sans serif letters without thick and thin lines.

The exemplar alphabets written with the B-Series nib shown above and below

Speedball

WRITING THE FUTURE'S HISTORY
B- Series nib, Michael Clark

illustrate the ductus of traditional, uniform-width letterforms.

The B-Series nib can be used for a variety of monoline lettering (see *Monoline* section pages 32-37), drawn letters (such as *Versals*, pages 56-58) and "*built-up*" letters such as the *Double Stroke Poster Roman* shown opposite page.

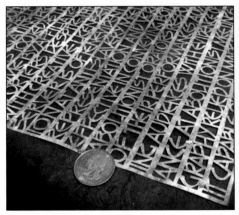

Lettered with a B-Series nib and then cut out of paper, Julie Gray

Broken strokes show construction of "Beginner's" alphabet. Numbered arrows indicate the order and direction of elements. Made with B-Series Speedball. The Speedball Textbook, 11th Edition (1929).

Master Folk Artists

The lettering sample above uses the B-Series nib with pen manipulation (turning the pen at different angles to achieve thick and thin strokes while writing), Michael Clark

SPURRED GOTHIC
abcdefgh jklmno
pqrstuvwxyyzja
ABCDEFGHIJKLMN
OPQRSTUVWXYZ
1234567890$

A bold-faced alphabet of rapid, single-stroke construction, suitable for show card lettering. The original was made on a 10" x 14" card using the B-Series pen, size B-2. Spurs added with the same pen turned over on its back. The Speedball Textbook, 10th Edition (1927).

Double-Stroke Poster Roman
Letters Built-up with #4 Style "B" Speedball (Round Point) Pen
Note ► A close imitation of double-stroke lettering is produced by the single-stroke method using Style "D" Speedball (oval point) Pens.

abcdefg ABCDEF
hijklmn GHIJKLM
opqrstu NOPQRST
vwxyz& UVWXYZ

Double-Stroke lettering by William Hugh Gordon. The Speedball Textbook, 2nd Edition (1916).

C-SERIES FLAT

The third addition to the Speedball Series of pen nibs was introduced in 1918 in the 4th Edition of The Speedball Textbook. The C-Series nib is a traditional broad-edged nib with a great degree of flexibility. The nib's flexibility was intended to have similar characteristics to ancient scribes' reed pens while offering the lettering artist "a close imitation of the finest small brush work."

Used for traditional forms of calligraphy, this C-Series nib is held at a constant angle, although each alphabet has minor variations on this angle. This consistent pen angle will give the lettering artist the desired thick and thin strokes usually associated with broad-edged calligraphy.

A variety of effects can be made by manipulating the pen from this constant angle (see *Bone Alphabet*, pages 66-67).

The C-Series nib can be used to write any of the traditional calligraphic hands such as *Roman, Carolingian, Uncial, Italic, Gothicized Italic, Blackletter* or *Neuland*.

C-Series nib, Julian Waters

C-Series numbers featured in The Speedball Loose-Leaf System of Professional Lettering, Ross F. George.

24

MOVIE TITLES

made with the STYLE ~C~ Speedball Pen
Simplified Single Stroke Roman Construction in White Ink

ABCDEFGHIJKLMN
OPQRSTUVWXYZ
abcdefghijklmnopqrst
uvw $1234567890¢xyyz

This Alphabet beautifully radiates the Feminine Appeal
in "Daintiness, Gracefulness and Refinement"

C-Series nib with white ink on black board. The Speedball Textbook, 12th Edition (1933). This alphabet was the inspiration for "By George Titling" typeface on page 95.

Mufaro's Beautiful Daughters

AN AFRICAN TALE

John Stevens

The Speedball Textbook

Title lettering for 22nd and 23rd Editions of The Speedball Textbook (1991 & 1999), Julian Waters

for Specialty Posters
Where legibility is not paramount

STUNT ROMAN

Lettered with a Style "C" (size 5) Speedball Pen

a b c d e f g h i j k l n
m o p q r s s t u w
A B C D E F G H I K
J L M N V X Y Z P O Q S
R T U V W X Y Z ? &

The Speedball Textbook, 11th Edition (1929)

D - SERIES OVAL

The 1926 publication of the 9th Edition of The Speedball Textbook contained the first mentions of the D-Series nib in the *Metropolitan Poster* alphabet and the advertisement for the Style-D that appeared on the back inside cover.

This nib completed the Speedball Series of pen nibs. Its oval shape was ideal for smaller poster lettering because it produced a letter with an accentuated rounded-finish in the same character styles that could be executed with a C-Series nib.

The addition of the D-Series made for even bolder finishes on forms and enhanced the variety and dimension that a lettering artist could provide their clientele.

Today, the D-Style nib is no longer manufactured.

ALPHABETS CREATED FOR POSTERS WITH THE D-SERIES NIB

First Style-D alphabet example; The Speedball Textbook, 9th Edition (1926) and "Built Up Style-D Romans;" The Speedball Textbook, 12th Edition (1933).

STEEL BRUSH

In 1960, the 18th Edition of The Speedball Textbook introduced the Steel Brush into its array of lettering tools.

The purpose of using a Steel Brush is to make larger letters that cannot be made with a pen (one quarter inch is about as wide as a pen with a reservoir can be made and still function properly). The Speedball Steel Brush is dipped and used like a pen and has a very flexible tip. It performs the same functions as the conventional lettering brush, but with its seven staggered layers of steel and brass and its four interchangeable sizes, it allows for far more control than a lettering brush.

It can be used for larger lettering work such as posters or banners and is suitable for use with inks or paint. Because it is a wide tool, you can dip the Steel Brush into different colored inks and get some very interesting effects, such as changing colors within a letter or a word.

Any alphabet that is used with a broad-edged nib can be executed with a Steel Brush such as *Blackletter*, *Neuland*, or *Roman* capitals.

Steel Brushes range in size from ¼ inch to ¾ inch and allow you to make letters more than seven inches high.
The Speedball Textbook, 18th Edition (1960)

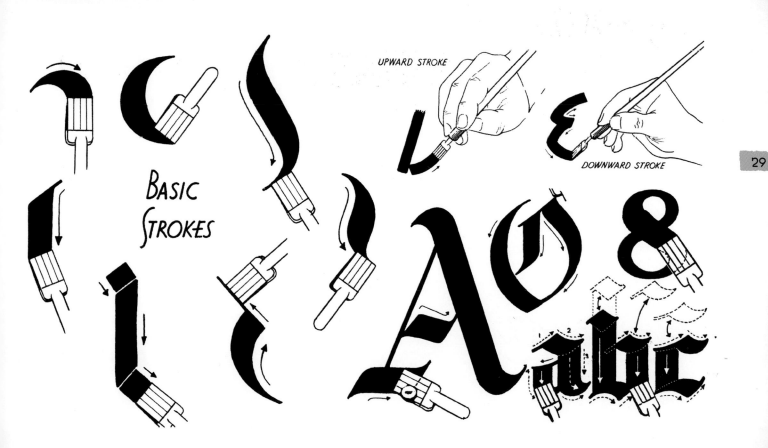

UPWARD STROKE

DOWNWARD STROKE

BASIC STROKES

ElegantWriter®

The Elegant Writer® calligraphy marker is an excellent broad-edged tool designed for the calligrapher. Because of the portability and ease of use, this tool makes the "thinking process" of calligraphy easy with no dipping, filling or problems with ink flow.

The chisel-edged nib glides easily, making strokes of any direction effortless and enables flourishing without the problems of snags and splatters.

Use the Elegant Writer as you would a normal broad-edged calligraphy pen, keeping the nib perpendicular to the upper left corner of the page (an approximate angle of 45°) for a ribbon-like quality line.

1.3mm	2.0mm	2.5mm	3.0 mm
Extra Fine	Fine	Medium	Bold

Elegant Writer markers are water-soluble and available in a variety of colors (black, blue, red, green, brown, gold and silver) and sizes (1.3mm, 2.0mm, 2.5mm, 3.0mm and 3.5mm).

LETTERING IDEAS

After writing with a broad-edged marker, outline the letters using a fine monoline marker in black or a contrasting color.

shadow

Add a shadow to the letters either on the right and bottom, or left and bottom, with a light color such as gray, pale blue or yellow.

bounce

Intentionally alternate the base line of every other letter to create motion.

rock

Change the pen angle to rock onto a corner of the marker nib to make fine lines and "feet" or serifs for each letter.

two-toned

Two-toned letters - repeat top or bottom halves of the letters with the same size marker in another color. This sample illustrates the use of the Elegant Writer in silver on top of black.

diamonds

Add a decorative touch with diamonds by turning the pen diagonally and making a diamond on the strokes of the letters.

Add dots with gold or silver metallic markers.

Color in the counter spaces as well as the negative spaces between letters and words with any type of contrasting markers or colored pencils. (Note: The color can touch the letters, or a slight space can be left between the letter and the color)

Dainty ~ ROMAN ~ Italics
for Grace, Elegance and Feminine Appeal

CLASSIC ROMAN
for Conservative Dignity, Permanence and Beauty

Texts · **Church Gothic** · **UNCIAL**
for Antiquity, Quality, Craftsmanship and Reverence

GOTHIC AND BLOCK
for Strength, Power and a Sturdy Atmosphere

"*Personality Script*"
for Commands, Quick Action, it speaks for itself!

The "JAZZY STYLES"
Frivolous Freedom effected by Broken line

RADIO CATERPILLAR CHINA SILKS ICE
for individuality, Novelty, Character Expression

MODERNistic ABC
for that Ultra-Modern Advertisement !!!

Advertising Moods first appeared in The Speedball Textbook, 13th Edition (1938).

Relatively few materials are needed to begin making letters; with paper, pen or brush and ink the world of lettering is available to anyone who is interested and willing to practice.

The styles in this section include a diverse array of hands that can be written with a variety of tools. Each alphabet has an exemplar showing how the letters are made, some information about that specific hand, and an example of how it can be used. Some of the sections contain additional variations on the alphabet.

Numerous alphabet styles have developed through the centuries; the examples on the following pages are often used today by designers, calligraphers and lettering artists.

Different lettering styles meet different needs, and it is important to be aware of the suitability of an alphabet for a given project. The look of a hand can set the mood for the viewer, so it is important to consider which lettering styles are a match for the design.

The images above are from one of the pages from the 14th Edition of the Speedball Textbook (1941) and illustrates some of the uses of lettering to create mood.

MONOLINE

The term "monoline," refers to a line of uniform width. For the student, writing with a monoline tool gives vital information about letter proportion and formation.

The exemplar on the opposite page, *Monoline with Round & Square Terminals*, shows the basic practice strokes that make up elements of the letters.

For a monoline that requires a square- or diamond-shaped finish, use the Speedball A-Series nibs and hold the pen upright (45°) with the shoe of the nib flat on the paper.

For letters requiring rounded-finish terminals (endings), use the Speedball B-Series.

The rounded nib of this series will result in the desired rounded ending regardless of the pen angle.

Both the A-Series nibs (sizes A-0 to A-6) and B-Series nibs (sizes B-0 to B-6) give a wide variety of creative possibilities, ranging from lightweight (*Architects & Draftsmen*, page 35) to bold (*Poster Gothic*, page 35) or decorative (*Vanitie Roman*, page 37 and *Versals*, pages 56-58).

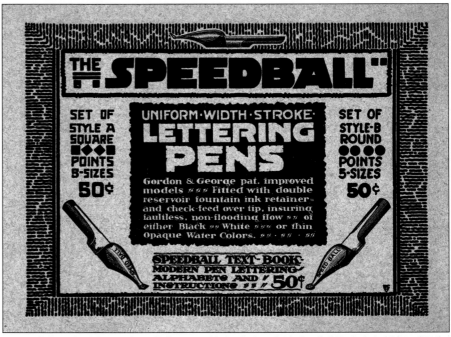

Originally lettered and drawn with Speedball pens using black and white ink. The Speedball Textbook, 2nd Edition (1916).

abcdefghijklmnopqrstuvwxyz & blocks

Gothic-style monoline letters. The Speedball Textbook, 2nd Edition (1916)

MONOLINE WITH ROUND & SQUARE TERMINALS

Numbered elementary principles. – The arrows indicate direction of drawing strokes →

NOTICE !
Overlap the strokes in joining all oval or circular elements.

Note – Elementary principles are identical in both round and square finished tips of all gothic letters.

Monoline (also known in the printing industry as Gothic) square terminals produced by the A-Series Speedball shown in red.
The rounded terminals shown in blue were lettered with the B-Series Speedball. 2nd Edition (1916).

Vertical Manuscript

ABCDEFGHIJKLMN
OPQRSTUVWXYZ&
1 2 3 $4 5 6 7 8 9 0

Practice several lines of each exercise before making letters.

ABCDEFGHIJJKLMNOPQRSTUTVWXYYZ&

Practice several lines of each exercise before making letters. This practice page first appeared in the 14th Edition of The Speedball Textbook by Ross F. George (1941)

POSTER GOTHIC

WITH STYLE 'B' SPEEDBALL PENS

ABCDEFGHI
JKLMNOPQT
RSUVWXYZ
$123456789¢

ABCDEFGHIJ

LETTERED WITH STYLE 'B' SPEEDBALL

KLMNOPQRS

RETOUCHED WITH A FINE PEN

TUVWXYZ&
1234567 8$9

Ross F. George, The Speedball Textbook, 12th Edition (1933)

A few Extra Numerals
B
123
456
789
$3.75
123¢
456
789

*The Speedball Textbook,
15th Edition (1948)*

ARCHITECTS & DRAFTSMEN
Rapid, single stroke alphabets with B-5 or B-6 Speedball

ABCDEFGHIJKM
LNOPQRSTUVW
XY$23456789¢Z?
abcdefghijklmnopq
a u
rstuvwxyz,&afgrsky
abcdefghijklmnopqrs
tuvwxyz vw and abefghsky
ABCDEFGHIJKLMS
NOPQRTUVWXYZJ
ABCDEFGHIJKLMNOPQRSST
UVWXYYZ$1234567890 3¢

Lettered with at B-5 Speedball pen. A bolder pen is not well suited for this style.
The Speedball Textbook, 6th Edition (1921)

abcdefghijklmn
A-0 nib

1920 rounded
A-3 nib

monoline
B-3 nib

abcdefghijklmnopqrstuvwxyz
A-3 nib

uncial round
B-3 nib

A SERIES LIGHT
A-3 nib

Roundational
B-3 nib

opqrstuvwxyz

Monoline sampler using A- and B-Series nibs, Randall Hasson

⁘DRAFTMAN'S ART⁘ FB·6 & COMPASS

HBCDEF,G
HIJKL?MN
OPQRSTU
VWWXYZ

This alphabet can also be made single-stroke with B-Series Speedball. The Speedball Textbook, 14th Edition (1941) and was the inspiration for typeface "Vertical Roundpoint JNL" on page 95.

VANITIE ROMAN

This revised alphabet uses two sizes of the B-Series nib. The Speedball Textbook, 16th Edition (1952) and originally appeared in the 11th Edition (1929).

Divinity Italics
69¢ per dozen
Different motifs for Poster Ornamentation can be taken from most any floral study
$2.43 50¢ ea.

Each letter in this alphabet was built up with monoline strokes using a B-Series nib. The Speedball Textbook, 12th Edition (1933).

CLASSIC ✦ ROMAN

A B C D E F G
H I J K L M N
O P Q R S T U
V X & Y ? W Z

Letters are outlined with #5 style "B"or"D" Speedball Pen, then filled-in

This alphabet was inspired by 2nd century chisled Roman letters found on the Trajan column. The characters J, U, W, E and ? did not appear in the early Roman alphabet. *The Speedball Textbook 11th Edition (1929).*

THE ROMAN ALPHABET

Excerpted from The Speedball Textbook, 17th Edition (1956) by Ross F. George

A B C D E K I

ANCIENT GREEK ALPHA   *LATIN*
Α A   A A   A
    LATER

ΑΛΗΘΩΥ
ΦΕ   *RANDOM LETTERS FROM
4TH. CENT. CODEX SINAITICUS*
    BY OLD REED PENS

SERUANT
AFMB   *RANDOM LETTERS FROM
6TH. CENT. CODEX BEZÆ*

ABVRU
e f g h k m
n r t u v w
a y   *IF YOU HAVE TOO MUCH SPACE AT END OF LINE, USE THESE PER-
MISSABLE EXTENSIONS FOR WORDS ENDING IN THESE LETTERS*

The *Roman* alphabet is both beautiful and useful. It lends itself to individual modifications and type innovations which are usually created simply by changing the design of the serif or by adding a few ornamental touches to the body of the letter.

In learning the *Single Stroke Roman*, (analyzed on pages 43 to 45) study the letters carefully before using the pen. Note where strokes start and end, their order of construction, and how the pen is manipulated in producing them.

Make a page of each letter, using a C-Series (C-2) pen. Try to combine a smooth arm movement with a flexible manipulation of the pen.

Next, make several pages of the full alphabets. Letters should be one inch high at first, ruling three guidelines for each line of copy. Keep the serifs as uniform as possible and try to equalize the space between letters as you work.

ROMAN CAPITALS with STYLE "C" SPEEDBALL PENS

NUMBERED ARROWS SHOW DIRECTION AND ORDER OF STROKES   (DOTTED CIRCULAR ARROWS SHOW TWIRLING OF PEN)

Grip the pen holder lightly and as closely to the marking tip as the holder permits, so that it can be twirled between thumb and index finger on difficult combination strokes.
The Speedball Textbook, 12th Edition (1933).

MODERN Single Stroke ROMAN
Style·C·Speedball

A rapid legible alphabet for Artists and Sho-card Writers.

(Ornamental numerals built up with small size pen)

a b c d e f g h i j k l m

a b c d e f g h i j k l m

n o p q r s t u w x y z

n o p q r s t u w x y z

$ 1 2 3 4 5 6 7 8 9 ¢

A rapid, single stroke show card alphabet that can be mastered with a little careful practice. Note that a flexible manipulation of the pen is recognized to produce the sharp, clean cut serifs and the finished elements in a single stroke. Do not overload the pen with ink. The Speedball Textbook, 11th Edition (1929).

POMPEIIAN WALL WRITING

The condensed Roman capital alphabet from Pompeii. The ductus, or stroke order.

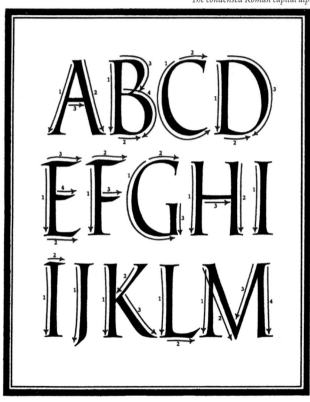

Reprinted from The Speedball Textbook, 21st Edition (1985), Cynthia Hollandsworth

ABCDEFG
HIJKLMN
OPQRST
UVWXYZ

SEMIFORMAL CAPITALS
Pen made capitals wth rotated serifs

This style has a different feel compared with styles with no variation in pen angle or pressure

Hh

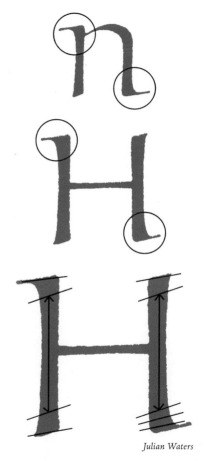

Julian Waters

ALPHABET STYLES

SINGLE-STROKE ROMAN

use the size of pen that will make the widest elements in one stroke

The Speedball Textbook, 15th Edition (1948)

abcdefg 123
hijklmno 456
pqrstuv 789
wxyz&a $ ©, ¢

The Speedball Textbook, 15th Edition (1948)

ALPHABET STYLES

SHOWING THE SPURRED X·Y·Z CONSTRUCTION OF GOTHIC WITH A DRY BRUSH STROKE

DOTTED ARROWS SHOW TWIRLING OF BRUSH   NUMBERED ARROWS SHOW STROKES

ABCDEFGH
IJKLMNOR
PQSTUVW&

Ross F. George, The Speedball Textbook, 12th Edition (1933)

Ross F. George, The Speedball Textbook, 12th Edition (1933)

John Stevens

ALPHABET STYLES

HOW TO MAKE FLAT BRUSH ROMAN CAPITALS

Structurally, *Roman* letterforms are based on a 30° angle and require the manipulation or turning of the brush to make the serif strokes.

Keeping the 30° structure in mind and in one continuous motion, the entry stroke for the vertical stem starts (almost) horizontal at 0°. Then, while pulling the stroke down, the angle changes to 30°, returning back to 0° to form the serif.

Hold the brush lightly between the two first fingers and thumb, holding the brush almost perpendicular to the page, keeping the tip in contact with the paper as the letter is drawn.

BRUSH ANGLES

There are three important brush angles to remember while making a *Roman* letter with a flat brush—0°, 30° and 90°.

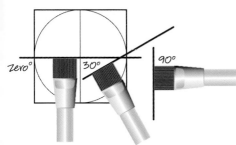

Zero°   *30°*   *90°*

The largest turn to master with a brush is a 1/4 turn.

Shape brush on palette.   *Work mostly on the tip.*

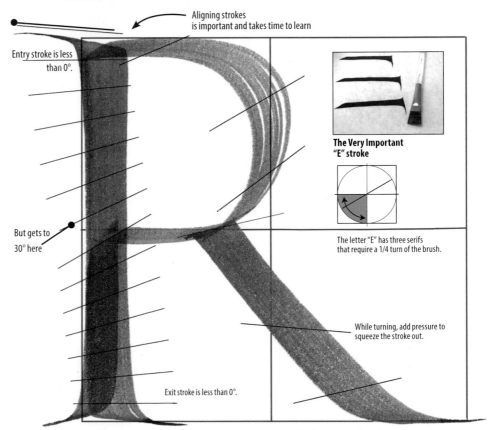

Aligning strokes is important and takes time to learn

Entry stroke is less than 0°.

But gets to 30° here

The Very Important "E" stroke

The letter "E" has three serifs that require a 1/4 turn of the brush.

While turning, add pressure to squeeze the stroke out.

Exit stroke is less than 0°.

Strokes are left translucent on the example to show the angle changes in each stroke.   *John Stevens*

Dick Beasley

Exceptions to 30° pen angle:
Capitals A, V, W, X, Y and small v, w, x, y are written at 40° pen angle.
First stroke of M and outside strokes of N at 55° pen angle.

Foundational

The *Foundational* hand is a simplified *Roman* form that was developed by English calligraphy revivalist, Edward Johnston, and published in his 1906 book, *Writing and Illuminating and Lettering.*

A broad-edged nib like the C-Series nib or Elegant Writer marker is used with a pen angle of 30° and an x-height of 4 pen widths. Majuscules are written at 6 pen widths high.

This hand is one of the most pleasing to write as one develops a rhythm with rounded entry and exit strokes. Many who teach lettering use this as an early model for their students because it is an extremely legible hand and also gives an understanding of the basic structure of many minuscule (lowercase) alphabets.

The serif is made in two strokes:

Eleanor Winters

ınnnmhkbpr Anb

Three Stroke "A"   Two Stroke "A"

vıuuy avaa adgq

ocegs lt f ij vwyyx z

ncndnenfngnhninj

Alternate "n" with every letter to establish a rhythm when practicing any style of lettering.

Italic lowercase groups to practice, Julian Waters

Italic

The word, "italic," is used historically to mean the calligraphic hands developed in the 15th century by Italian scribes during the Renaissance.

For commercial lettering artists of the early 20th century, "italic" meant any alphabet that was forward-slanted, a definition that still holds in modern day digital fonts.

Today, the *Italic* hand, with its graceful ascenders and descenders and flourished strokes, is what most people immediately think of when the term, "calligraphy" is used. Broad-edged tools like the Speedball A-Series nib (turned over on its back), C-Series nib, Elegant Writer marker and the Speedball fountain pen are used to write the Italic hand.

A common x-height is 5 nib widths, and the pen angle most often used is between 30° and 40°. Ascender and descender guidelines can be drawn about 4 nib widths from the waist line and base line of the letter, if desired, for consistency.

Italic Capitals

52

Julian Waters

Italic Alphabets

a b c d e f g g h i j k l m n

o p q r s t u v w x y y z &

A B C D E F G H I J K L M &

CAPS: MOSTLY 25°

N O P Q R S T U V W X Y Z

Julian Waters

ALPHABET STYLES

Italic Handwriting

Italic Handwriting may be written with a small-sized, broad-edged dip pen, fountain or cartridge pen, calligraphic marker or any monoline tool.

Since the early 1900's there has been a growing interest in *Italic Handwriting* in the United States and across the globe.

It is an extremely legible, fast and flowing hand and a perfect choice for everyday use.

All letters written in one stroke unless otherwise indicated.

Join all lowercase letters, except lift before f and z, and lift after g, j, q and y.

Getty-Dubay

Fantastic Flourishes

Composition of a Flourish

s-curve spiral scallop loop ribbon

Flourishing zone

the   the   the   the

- Layout the flourish by first sketching in pencil, stemming from a stroke of the letter. Practice on tracing paper helps.
- Carefully ink in the order suggested.
- Erase the exposed pencil once ink is dry.

the the the the the

opt age age aye aye

Angelic

Calligraphy

Thank You

abcdefghijklm
nopqrstuvwxyz

A B G H K
N L O T V
W X Y Z

Ornaments

Holly Monroe

ALPHABET STYLES

Draw the vertical with a slight curve. This is known as "waisting." Lilli Wronker

VERSALS

Built-up and elaborately drawn *Roman* or *Lombardic* letters that are placed at a chapter opening or at the beginning of an important section of text are referred to as *Versals*.

In medieval times, some *Versals* were particularly ornate and included tiny illustrations that corresponded to the text in the manuscript in an effort to help illiterate people understand content.

Versals can be simply inked (as shown at the beginning of this text), gilded and burnished with gold leaf, and/or embellished with color and decoration, as shown on the opposite page.

Because these letterforms are drawn and then decorated, use smaller pen nibs, like the Speedball B-6 or C-6, to draw the outlines, then create the embellishments of color and pattern decoration inside the letter in a series of strokes.

"B" Versal drop cap, Gemma Black

egin with an outline in pencil, then ink the outline and fill in the centers after the outlines are completely dry.

Delicate outlines and patterns are best drawn with the small Crow Quill No. 102 or Hawk Quill No. 107 pointed pen nibs.

A good formula to establish the size for the basic *Versal* form is to make the letters 8 to 10 times taller than the width of the stem. See *Versal* alphabet exemplars on this page and the page opposite.

Contemporary examples of drawn *Versal* letters are shown on page 115 in the *Decorative Lettering* section.

Illuminated "B" Versal drop cap, Marian Gault

ABCDEFG
HIJKLᵐMN
OPQRST
U?VₑWXYZ

Ross F. George, The Speedball Textbook, 14th Edition (1941)

VERSALS
UNCIAL GOTHIC

Outlined with a   #5 Style "B"   Speedball Pen
This alphabet is used for ornamental initials in engrossments

The Speedball Textbook, 11th Edition (1929)

Azalea Buttercup Clematis Dandelion Eremophila Foxglove Geranium Hebe Impatiens Jasminum Knotweed Larkspur Magnolia Nasturtium Oleander Periwinkle Quince Rosemary Sunflower Tullium Umbrella Violet Wisteria Xeranthemum Yarrow Zinnia

PACIFIC STATES
FLORAL ALPHABET

Yukimi Annand

ALPHABET STYLES

x height = 2½ - 2⅔ nib widths

pen-angle = 20°

3-4 x heights interlinear space

f is shorter above and below

serif construction

"crossover" point for arched letters

• pen-angle for thick diagonals = 35°

trelictaciuitatenazareth uenit ethabitauit inc

naum mariamam.infinib: zabulon etnepthalir

adimpletetur quoddicium épetefaia prophet

Example from a 9th century manuscript

Sheila Waters

carolingian

Carolingian is an important part of lettering history as the first minuscule hand. Developed in 9th century France, this alphabet spread quickly under the reign of King Charlemagne due to its small size, rounded forms and ease of writing. *Carolingian* is a wide-lettered alphabet, written at a forward slant, with tall ascenders and clubbed serifs.

To write *Carolingian*, use the broad-edged Speedball C-Series nib, Elegant Writer marker or Speedball fountain pen. A common x-height is approximately 2 ½ nib widths with a constant, shallow pen angle of 20° to 25°.

The *interlinear space* (the space between lines) is 3 to 4 x-heights which will create a light and airy texture in a block of writing.

Use *Roman* or *Uncial forms* for corresponding capitals.

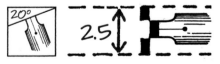

20°   2.5

UNCIAL

The word "uncial" is used historically to mean the calligraphic hands developed in the 2nd and 3rd centuries.

Uncial is a rounded, majuscule hand that was derived from *Roman* capitals. It served as the primary book hand between the 4th and 6th centuries and was used for headings until the Middle Ages.

In this capital style alphabet, the D, H, K and L have very short ascenders and there are slight descenders on F, G, P, Q and Y.

Initial letter from Shaws Book of Ornamental Letters, 1883.
The Speedball Textbook, 21st Edition (1985)

ABCDEFGHI
JKLMNOPQ
RSTUVWXY

CELTIC ROMAN   WITH   C-3 SPEEDBALL PEN

abcdefghijklmn
opqrstuvwxyz

The Speedball Textbook, 20th Edition (1972)

ROMAN UNCIAL

ABCDEFGHIJKLMN

OPQRSTUVWXYZ

ADKNWXY

Marsha Brady

To write *Uncial*, use the broad-edged C-Series nib, Elegant Writer or Speedball Fountain pen.

A common x-height is between 4 to 6 nib widths with a constant shallow pen angle of 20° to 25°. The exemplar above is based on a 5th century *Roman Uncial*, with x-height of 4 ½ pen widths and a 20° pen angle.

Note:
Artists should avoid the tendency to try to condense this script.

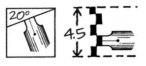

ALPHABET STYLES

GREEK UNCIAL

adapted from Codex Sinaiticus,
c. AD 350.

Α Β Γ Δ Ε Ζ Η Θ Ι

alpha beta gamma delta epsilon zeta eta theta iota

Κ Λ Μ Ν Ξ Ο Π Ρ C

kappa lambda mu nu xi omicron pi rho sigma +

Τ Υ Φ Χ Ψ Ω

tau upsilon phi chi psi omega

60°

pen angle varies from 0° to 60°

Georgia Angelopoulos

HEBREW

The root of the *Hebrew* letter styles we know today began around 300 BC with the appearance of the *Hebrew Square Script* – a version of which was found in the Dead Sea Scrolls. There are numerous styles of *Hebrew* calligraphy, from formal square letterforms to cursive script and cultural variations.

While written and read from right to left, the individual strokes comprising each letter are formed from left to right and from top to bottom, using a broad-edged tool like the Speedball C-Series nib.

Hebrew letters are usually written between 3 and 4 nib widths. Since greater emphasis is placed on the horizontal strokes of each letter, a relatively steep 60° pen angle is used. Because of this, many right-handed calligraphers find it preferable to write with left-handed nibs like Speedball's Left-handed C-Series.

The exemplar at the right is a variation on a basic *Foundational Script* that also shares many characteristics of form with the historical *Shephardic Script*. This form has a serifed lead-in stroke and subtle curves to the vertical strokes.

Izzy Pludwinski

63

NEULAND

Neuland is a bold lettering style that was developed by German calligrapher and type designer, Rudolf Koch, in the early 1900s. The characters in this alphabet have no thin strokes. *Neuland* is written at 4 to 5 pen widths high and can be used to form a dense texture on the page.

Both the Speedball A-Series and C-Series nib can create this alphabet. The C-Series requires a slight twisting and turning or *pen manipulation*, where the nib must constantly change between a 0° and 90° pen angle to form the curved and diagonal strokes. Because of its flexibility, the C-Series makes flared beginning and ending terminals when

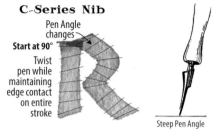

C-Series Nib

Pen Angle changes

Start at 90°

Twist pen while maintaining edge contact on entire stroke

Steep Pen Angle

slight pressure is applied, creating more character in the letter itself. This diagram illustrates the pen angle changes during vertical, curved and diagonal strokes. Refer to the exemplar shown on the opposite page for the suggested stroke

A-Series Nib

Pen Angle

Maintain constant pen angle throughout stroke

sequence to draw the letters.

To write with no pen manipulation, the A-Series makes *Neuland* style letters with a simple change of pen angle on curved and diagonal strokes.

When using the A-Series, the shoe of the nib must maintain contact with the paper for each stroke. The curves and diagonals are created by simply shifting the direction of the pen to 40°.

Poster Alphabet, Ross F. George, back cover of The Speedball Textbook, 12th Edition (1933)

Neuland style using a flat edge tool like the C-Series nib. Strokes require twisting and turning through each stroke, Karen Charatan

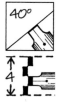

A-Series nib

THE QUICK BROWN FOX
JUMPED OVER THE LAZY DOGS

Neuland style using an A-Series nib. Strokes are manipulated differently from standard flat edge pens, Randall Hasson

ALPHABET STYLES

Bone Alphabet

Bone is written at an x-height of 3 nib widths with short ascenders and descenders to achieve dense texture.

Let the letters touch and tangle to create more closed counter spaces, which give a sparkle to the page.

Hold the pen vertically (as perpendicular to the page as is possible) to achieve the bone-like shape of the strokes.

The branching strokes on b, h, m, r and p begin below the center, inside the stem and at a very steep pen angle.

Keep the points of v, w, y and z slightly rounded.

The letter "e" is written entirely with a 30° angle.

Steep Angle

Carol DuBosch

abcdef
ghijkl
mnopq
rstuvw
xyz

1234567890

We
must
get in
touch
with
our own
liberating
ludicrousness
and
practice
being
harmlessly
insane

Carol DuBosch

ALPHABET STYLES

blackletter

Blackletter is one of many names used for the *Gothic* styles of lettering and refers to the dense texture and tightly-spaced vertical strokes of the minuscule letters for which it is known.

Blackletter can be written with the Speedball A-0 or A-1 (turned over on its back), C-0 or C-1, or other broad-edged tool.

The most common x-height is 4 ½ to 5 ½ nib widths (*Blackletter* should be written at no fewer than 4 nib widths), with a pen angle of 30° to 45° (adjustments in pen angle can alter the weight of the down stroke, making it either lighter or heavier, depending on angle).

ABCDEFGH
IJKLMNOP
QRSTUVWX
YZ Speedball
1234567890

Ward Dunham

Ward Dunham

In historical terms of calligraphy, the term Gothic refers to lettering styles such as Blackletter. In the commercial lettering of the early 19th century, the term Gothic was used by printers to mean letters of uniform width throughout the strokes.

ALPHABET STYLES

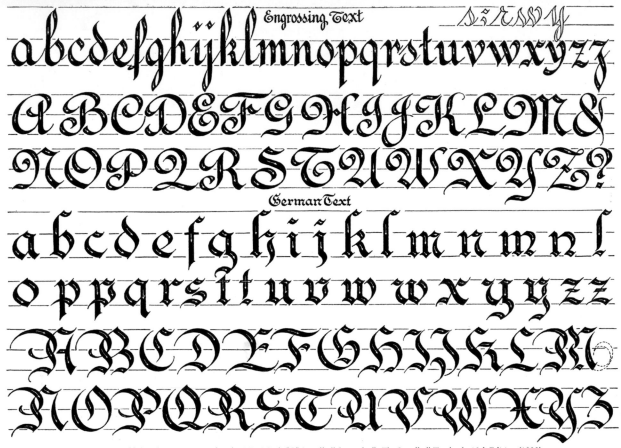

Engrossing Text

German Text

Original lettered on a 9 x 14 card with a No. 2 Style "C" Speedball (retouched), The Speedball Textbook, 12th Edition (1933)

Luca Barcellona

ALPHABET STYLES

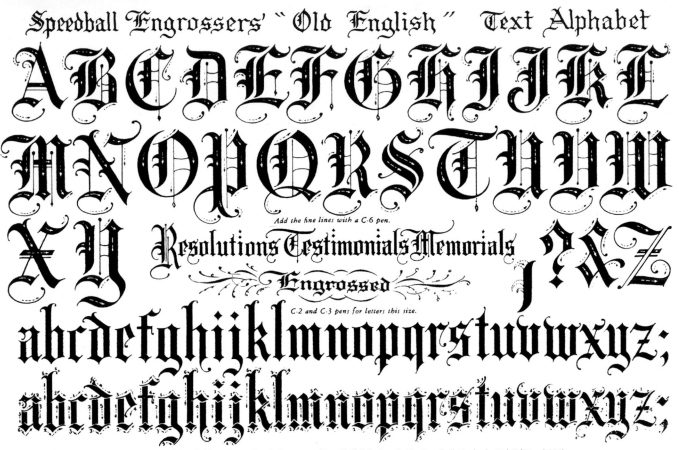

Speedball Engrossers' "Old English" Text Alphabet

A B C D E F G H I J K L
M N O P Q R S T U V W
X Y

Add the fine lines with a C-6 pen.

Resolutions Testimonials Memorials
Engrossed

C-2 and C-3 pens for letters this size.

J ? & Z

abcdefghijklmnopqrstuvwxyz;

abcdefghijklmnopqrstuvwxyz;

Engrossers' "Old English" text lettered with three sizes of Speedball C-Series nib, The Speedball Textbook, 12th Edition (1933)

Modified Text | for Pen or Brush

The Old | English

made with dry brush | to show construction

Dotted arrows show twirling of brush

Copyrights Reserved by Ross F. George, Seattle, U.S.A (including methods of showing strokes) 1933

The Speedball Textbook, 12th Edition (1933)

73

Gothicized Italic

Based on an early 14th century *Blackletter*, this richly decorative lettering style was developed by Edward Johnston in 1924. It combines the elements of a narrow *Foundational* style and because of its compressed and pointed character, *Gothicized Italic* has the lively rhythm of *Italic* when written on a slight slope.

To create, use the broad-edged Speedball C-Series nib, A-Series nib (turned over on its back), Speedball fountain pen, or Elegant Writer marker at a 40° pen angle.

This alphabet is written mostly upright but can be written with a slight forward slant.

The x-height is normally 5 nib widths, with the ascending and descending letters at 7 ½ nib widths and capitals at 6 nib widths high.

Add interest and character to this hand by using hairline strokes.

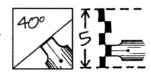

aabcddefffgg
hħijkklmno
pqrrsstuvv
wwxxyyzzz

Barry Morentz

74

FLAT BRUSH

The beauty of brush writing is in the subtle weight changes made by adding or releasing pressure during a stroke, as well as revealing the texture of the paper. The corners of the brush strokes can appear crisper if slightly exaggerated.

To write with a brush, find a comfortable position for your hand that allows for precise control of pressure on the end of the brush, while the bristles of the brush approach the paper almost completely vertically.

Some artists maintain contact with the paper using the little finger, edge of the hand, or wrist resting on the writing surface, while others let their hand move through the air touching only the tip of the brush to the paper.

A brush stroke with any thickness is usually pulled since the brush will resist being pushed against its bristles, except by those with the lightest of touches. Thin, sideways strokes, created by the edge of the brush, can go either direction.

Carl Rohrs

Father Edward Catich

RAPID BRUSH SHO CARD X·Y·Z SINGLE STROKE GOTHIC

·DOTTED ARROWS SHOW WAY BRUSH IS TWIRLED IN ACTION·

→ NUMBERED ARROWS SHOW MOVEMENT OF STROKES ←

A B C D E F G H I
J K L M N O P Q
R S T U V W ? &

HOW TO HOLD A BRUSH

Use No. 12 red sable sho-card brush with round ferrule. Hold it between thumb and index finger.

Ross F. George - The Speedball Textbook, 12th Edition (1933)

ALPHABET STYLES

Ross F. George - The Speedball Textbook, 13th Edition (1938)

ALPHABET STYLES

This section includes lettering styles that use varying degrees of pressure to create a letter with a pointed pen nib, brush, pencil and some small sized broad-edged nibs.

POINTED PEN PRINCIPLES

An oblique pen holder is used to write most pointed pen styles of lettering and is held with a 3-point grip.

Grasp the pen holder between the thumb and index finger as the pen rests on the side of the middle finger between the first joint or knuckle, and the end of the finger.

The thumb is placed on the pen so that it touches the offset flange.

Some people prefer to grasp their oblique holder in such a way so that the thumb merely touches the flange; others prefer to rest their thumb on top of the flange. Either way is correct, as long as the writer

has control to move the point as desired. Hold the pen with comfortable, non-fatiguing grip without excessive pressure.

PROPORTION

The standard "rule of thumb" of proportion for letters in writing with a pointed pen is determined by the writer.

This concept centers on the scale, or perspective, of how much taller the capital letters should be relative to the lowercase letter.

Traditionally, the capitals should be written at least 4-5 times the height of the shorter lowercase.

Copperplate or *Roundhand* capitals (page 84) are usually written at this height relationship. In *Spencerian Script* (page 80), a more spontaneous style, the capital letters are composed of large, exaggerated ovals and curves, producing an over-sized capital height and width which can exceed this traditional height relationship and can be as much as 8 to 10 times taller than the lowercase.

When writing ornamental penmanship (flourished *Spencerian*), larger capitals

Flourished Spencerian, Michael Sull

inherently possess very large, shaded strokes that are created by pressure, called shades (thicker strokes). These strokes are essential to the style and without them, the capitals would appear visually weak.

The shades create an essential visual balance in contrast to the lowercase and are a key element in maintaining the overall legibility of the letter, and the word it appears in.

Lighter pressure produces less flexing of the tines, creating thinner strokes. The finest hairline strokes are created on the upstrokes and horizontal strokes.

Thick lines are created on down strokes by pushing down on the nib, causing the nib tines to splay and allowing more ink to flow through the widened slit onto the writing surface.

78

POINTED PEN EXERCISES

The exercises on this page are fun to do while encouraging the practice of pressure and release and creating designs with the pointed nib.

For this project use: pencil, eraser, paper, Speedball Oblique Pen Holder, Hunt No. 56 Pen Nib, and drawing ink (your choice).

Even Pressure

Press & Release

More Practice Options

To begin, practice making pressure and release marks.

Lightly draw with a pencil a basic outline of a shape (e.g. square, circle, tree, flower, etc.).

Next, fill in the outline with your flexible pointed pen using thick and thin strokes, swirls, flourishes or ovals looping back and forth.

Lastly, erase the pencil lines once ink is completely dry.

TIP: Use light pressure for upward strokes and heavier pressure for downward strokes. Create flourishes by drawing light lines over either light or heavy lines, but never cross two heavy lines. Doing so will interrupt the graceful flow of your design.

Note: It may be preferred to place a sheet of the penciled outline on a light table and cover with a clean sheet of paper. This approach eliminates the need for an eraser.

Linda Schneider

PRESSURIZED LETTERING

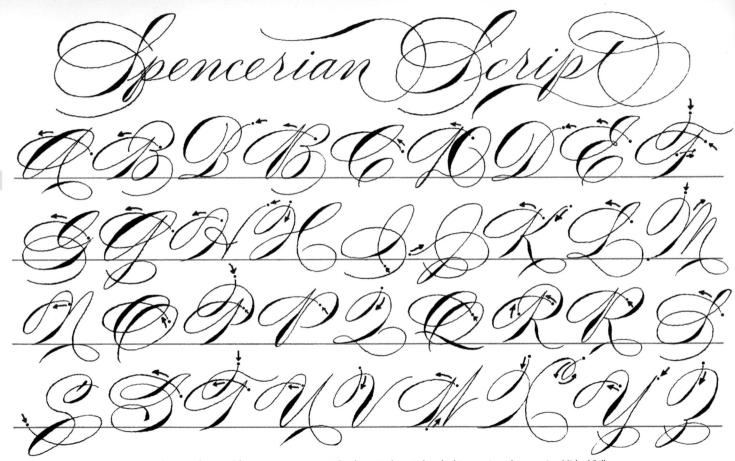

A combination of wrist and forearm movements are employed to write the capitals and achieve consistent letter spacing, Michael Sull

PRESSURIZED LETTERING

a b c d e f f g g h

i j j k l m n o p p

p p q q r s t t u v

w x y y z z

ending forms:

d r t
(d) (r) (t)

1 2 3 4 5 6 7 8 9 0 ! ? ; : ( )

Michael Sull

Spencerian Script letters slant at 52° from the base line. Finger muscles are used to write the lowercase letters. The pen point is used to create the thin hairline and bold shaded strokes. After the point is dipped in ink, move the pen on the paper with just enough pressure exerted upon the pen so that it glides on the paper for a very thin monoline stroke. However, when pressure is applied to the point while writing, the two tines of the point spread apart, opening a gap between the points releasing the writing fluid onto the paper, resulting in a wide stroke, called a "shade."

Strokes of varying lengths and widths are produced by controlling the degree of pen pressure.

American Cursive Handwriting

Aa Bb Cc Dd Ee Ff
Gg Hh Ii Jj Kk Ll Mm
Nn Oo Pp Qq Rr Ss
Tt Uu Vv Ww Xx Yy Zz

Numerals: 1 2 3 4 5 6 7 8 9 0 ! ? . , ; : ( ) ' ' " "

DECORATED CAPITALS

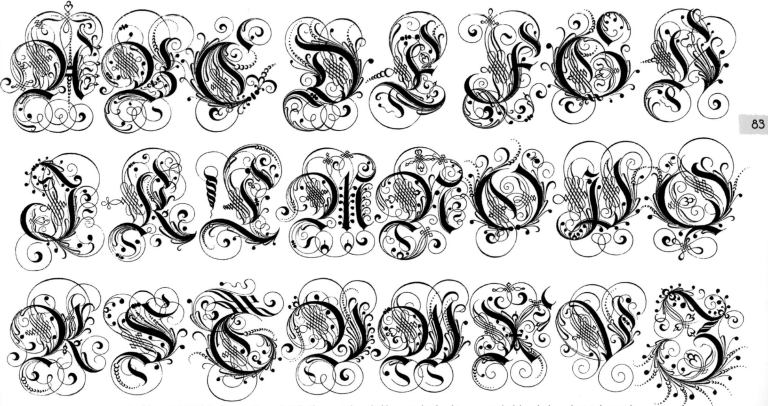

An example of decorated initials by Thomas Weston (1682). These capitals are highly manipulated and incorporates both broad-edge and pointed pen tools.

Roundhand Script

A B C D E F G H I J K L M

N O P Q R S T U V W X Y Z

A B C D E F G H I J K L M

N O P Q R S T U V W X Y Z

1234567890

a b c d e f g h i j k l m n o p q r s t u v w x y z z

a b c d e f g h i j k l m n o p q r s t u v w x y z z

This alphabet was published in the 12th Edition of The Speedball Textbook (1935) as an Engrossing Script. It was also published in the 11th Edition (1929) as a Roundhand Script.

Principles and letters - Roundhand Script

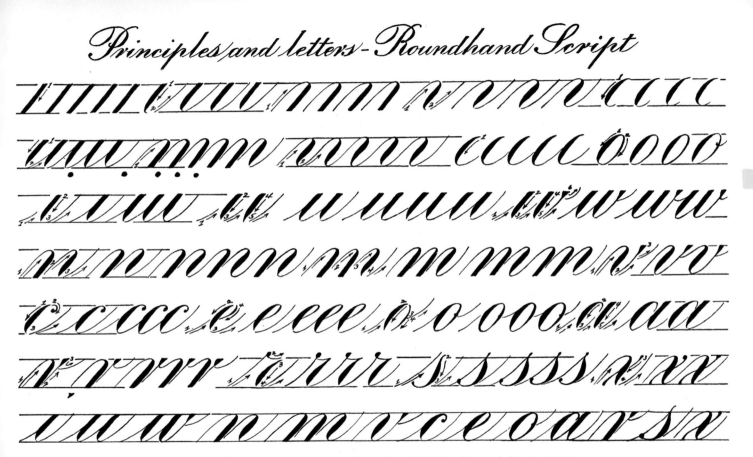

Lowercase Roundhand is a pointed pen style that was featured in the 11th Edition of The Speedball Textbook (1929).

Pointed Pen Variations

abcdefghijklmnopqrstuvwxyz

1234567890

ABCDEFGHIJKLM

NOPQRSTUVWXYZ

1234567890

Mike Kecseg

PRESSURIZED LETTERING

abcdefghijklmnopqrstuvwxyz

abcdefghijklmnopqrstuvwxyz

abcdefghijklmnopqrstuvwxyz

abcdefghijklmnopqrstuvwxyz

abcdefghijklmnopqrstuvwxyz

A progression of pen variations, Mike Kecseg

PRESSURIZED LETTERING

Listen

Barbara Calzolari

Growing in the garden of your beautiful Spirit

Kathy Milici

Yukimi Annand

Nicole Kristine Kikuchi and Michael Scott Ueda

Janet Takahashi

Scout Leaders' Wives

Cliff Mansley

88

PRESSURIZED LETTERING

Contemporary

Mike Kecseg

Mike Kecseg

Jake Weidmann

Jake Weidmann

PRESSURIZED LETTERING

The pointed brush offers lettering artists great flexibility and freedom. One brush can be manipulated to create many diverse styles and weights. Use a round, fine pointed watercolor brush that is resilient and springy. There are many brushes to choose from: sable or synthetic brushes, cartridge brush pens, oriental brushes, and fiber tip brush markers. Every brush will give a slightly different effect.

A brush handles differently than a broad-edged pen because it does not have a fixed width. The thickness of the stroke is determined by varying the amount of pressure which produces a line that can change from thick to thin in one continuous stroke.

Like a pen, a brush should be held lightly but firmly between the thumb and the first two fingers. Unlike the finger motions used to write with a pen, brush letters are formed by using a relaxed whole arm and wrist movement.

Strive for consistency in the thick and thin strokes; slight pressure is applied for the thick down strokes, and then lessened for thinner upstrokes. The upstrokes are

Stroke instruction, Judy Kastin. *The Speedball Textbook, 22nd Edition (1991).*

done with the brush held more upright (vertical) to the page. Practice is necessary to develop a rhythm, which helps maintain even stroke weight.

The pointed brush is an extremely versatile tool, ideal for doing fluid, continuous flourishes. It lends itself naturally to contemporary styles, and is often used for sign work, logo designs, headlines, and all types of casual, informal lettering.

Pointed brush letters created in preparation for Alpine Script font on page 95, Charles Borges de Oliveira

Use the side of the brush while applying pressure for heavier weight down strokes and the less pressure for thinner strokes, Karen Charatan

PRESSURIZED LETTERING

Pointed Brush Script

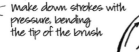

Pause

Pull down

Pause

Make down strokes with pressure, bending the tip of the brush

Make up strokes with little pressure using the tip of the brush.

Pull down and release pressure for dot

Make "v" and "w" in separate strokes that overlap at the bottom.

on curved descenders – g, j, y push left while quickly releasing pressure

Take the first thin up stroke all the way to the top on "a" and related letters d, g, q

Make "o" in one stroke or in two strokes.

Taper the bottom bowl on "b" and "p" by releasing pressure and pushing left

Make left-to-right diagonal strokes by holding the brush above the stroke

Make horizontal strokes by holding the brush under the stroke

Eliza A. Holliday and Marilyn Reaves

Terminals
Beginnings & Endings

Blunt — n

Blunt — n

Swing in — n

Pull in — n

Blunt — n

Flick down — n

Curve — n

ink — Blunt

ink — Curve

ink — Curve

ink — Taper Curve

ink — Sharp

ink — Flick up

ink — Reverse Curve

Marilyn Reaves

PRESSURIZED LETTERING

LETTERING WITH GRAPHITE

Pressure & Release Pencil Caps

The attractive *waisting* (tapered line quality) found on all strokes in this alphabet is produced by the technique of *Pressure and Release*.

The straight strokes almost always start and end with dense pressure, the round strokes begin with the lightest touch before applying a gradual pressure and then finally releasing your touch. Try the exercises below using a soft 2B or 4B pencil to get familiar with pressure and release strokes.

A textured paper with tooth creates a textured mark while developing the important sensitivity of touch, that is necessary in lettering.

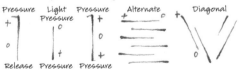

While this technique may not be 'easy' at first, it is worth the effort to practice, as most of the pencil strokes transfer directly to conventional pen letters.

A B C D E F G H
I J K L M N O P R
S T U V W X Y & Z
V O O I E S P

Peter Thornton

Wren

Graphite and watercolor, Amity Parks

PRESSURIZED LETTERING

LETTERING FOR FONTS

Many fonts have been digitized to emulate the essence of hand lettering.

The first step in designing a typeface or font family is to establish a clear vision of its purpose.

* Determine if the letters are serif or sans serif (without serifs).
* Is it going to be used for display or text?
* Is it a bold or condensed face, modular or organic?
* Will the typeface include ligatures, extended characters and/or ornaments, frames, flourishes and monograms?

Extended characters are set with a single key stroke Cantoni Pro collection by Debi Sementelli

Imagine what the typeface might look like, the feel and how to get the nature of the hand-lettered strokes from paper to font design software glyph cell.

A typeface should contain a full set of upper- and lowercase letters, numbers and special characters.

Alternate characters available in the font "Gratitude" by Kathy Milici.

The next step is to draw the letterforms. Some designers start with pencil and begin writing pages of letter styles before working digitally, while others build their letterforms directly with software using a tablet or mouse.

Pencil drawings for the typeface Villa by Larry Brady

Begin by drawing some core lowercase letters (such as o, u, h and n), building curves, lines and shapes that will reappear throughout the font.

Determine the *branching* technique of each letter. See page 16 for *points of tangency* and *points of intersection* branching methods.

The letters in a typeface are distinct from each other, yet they share many attributes, such as x-height, line weight, slant of the letter, pen angle and letter proportions.

Spacing and *kerning* in any typeface are critical elements that define the nature of the typeface. This time-consuming task is controlled by adding blank areas next to each character as well as creating kerning pairs that determine the distance between particular characters.

Writing out many pages of hand-lettered character combinations, numerals and variations is suggested in order to fine-tune the lettering and to satisfy the required elements of joining, spacing and kerning that is necessary in the font building process.

Since making a font involves vector graphics (using points, lines and curves) for scalability to almost any size, the number of anchor points used to form a character can present a challenge for the designer.

Sometimes what begins as an idea for a typeface may end up looking quite different, as shown in the example on the opposite page.

The word,
and each
of its
constituent
parts,

Hand-lettering prior to digitizing

the word
and each
of its
constituent
parts,

"Sweepy" by Michael Clark

sting · abcdefghijklmnopqrstuvwxyz

P22 Foundry by Michael Clark. This typeface contains 12 alternate lowercase characters.

VERTICAL ROUNDPOINT JNL
ABCDEFGHIJKLMNOPQRSTUVWXYZ

Redrawn digitally by Jeff Levine from the Draftman's Art featured on page 36.

By George Titling
ABCDEFGHIJKLMNOPQRSTUVWXYZ
abcdefghijklmnopqrstuvwxyz

Nick's Fonts by Nick Curtis. Inspired by the Movie Titling alphabet featured on page 25.

Alpine Script · Aa Bb Cc Dd Ee Ff Gg Hh Ii Jj Kk Ll Mm Nn Oo Pp Qq Rr Ss Tt Uu Vv Ww Xx Yy Zz

Borges Lettering by Charles Borges de Oliveira. This typeface contains 29 alternate characters.

STEVENS TITLING · ABCDEFGHIJKLMNOPQRSTUVWXYZ

Linotype® by John Stevens and Ryuichi Tateno. Four fonts in the suite are named after animals — Badger, Boar, Sable and Wolf.

Cantoni Pro · Aa Bb Cc Dd Ee Ff Gg Hh Ii Jj Kk Ll Mm Nn Oo Pp Qq Rr Ss Tt Uu Vv Ww Xx Yy Zz

Debi Sementelli Type Foundry by Debi Sementelli. This typeface contains 1265 glyphs and is available in Bold.

FUN & GAMES JNL · ABCDEFGHIJKLMNOPQRSTUVWXYZ

Fun and Games JNL was redrawn digitally by Jeff Levine from the lettering found on the cover of the 12th Edition (1933). See page 64.

SIGN PAINTING

In the early 20th century, sign painters produced not only large scale lettering for walls, bulletins, vehicles, windows, and other retail signage, but also smaller scale lettering for display cards used by merchants. Small lettering was tedious to execute with brushes, and eventually a specialized branch of sign painting called "show card" writing arose. Interior signs, such as show cards, are normally viewed from not much farther away than arm's length. Exterior signs, by comparison, are viewed from less-predictable distances and need to be designed accordingly.

Gordon and George invented the Speedball nib to increase the speed of show card work, and The Speedball Textbook was born out of the need for an instructional guide for the use of their commercial lettering pens. Today, many sign artists credit The Speedball Textbook as being their first lettering resource and an important part of their library.

Contemporary sign artists use paint, gold leaf, and other materials to achieve an astonishing array of effects.

Pencil drawing on paper for a glass panel, Noel Weber

Hand-lettered sign on primed wood, using One-Shot lettering enamels, Mark Oatis

Brush-lettered and airbrushed twentieth anniversary
artwork for Letterheads, Mark Oatis

Glass-gilded A over an acid-etched center, outlined in black.
Transparent glaze and blended color for added dimension.
Noel Weber

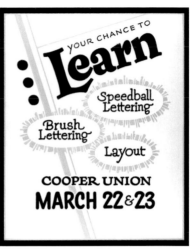

Brush-lettered and Speedball pen lettered card
sign for a workshop, John Downer

Touched up with white tempera in a
red sable brush, John Downer

Acrylic paint on wood, lettering and effects painted with matte acrylic on Masonite. Logo screen printed in clear tinted gloss. Tom Seibert

COMICS

The Speedball nib has a long history of use in comic art. For the lettering in the dialogue balloons, sound effects and titles, artists often use the B-Series, C-Series or the Hunt No. 107 nibs.

Cartoonists have also employed Speedball as drawing tools as well. In the artwork at right, a dip pen was used to create an appearance similar to an animation cel, with the characters stylistically differentiated from the backgrounds.

The characters are inked with Speedball B-Series nibs in order to give them a heavier and less organic line quality than the scenic elements, for which more flexible nibs, like the Hunt No. 101, are used.

Speedball D-Series nibs are occasionally used for long thick-and-thin curves and the C-Series nibs for panel borders and other ruled lines.

98

A variety of traditional dip pens are used to achieve a wide range of line quality. Jim Woodring

Lettering by award-winning artist, Todd Klein

DISPLAY LETTERING

Chalkboard displays are modern versions of show cards, most often used today by retailers and restaurants.

Many of these are done quickly and are temporary – when the sale is over, they can be erased and/or painted over to be re-used again.

In addition to chalk, some lettering artists use paint pens for a quick and easy tool to obtain vibrant colors and allow for the use of more traditional lettering techniques.

Chalk can be layered over painted letters, and surfaces can be anything from traditional chalkboards to hardboard purchased from the hardware store and painted with either chalkboard or black floor paint.

Paint pen on blackboard, Katherine Malmsten

Chalk on blackboard, Katherine Malmsten

Traditional pen and brush-lettered displays, Karen Charatan

CHALKBOARD LETTERING

Create large eye-catching signs by taking a design and enlarging it proportionately to the sign area.

You'll need: pencil, layout paper, chalk, chalkboard, yard/meter stick, mahlstick and your design to scale up.

STEP 1 - Create your design, layout on a grid or use Bienfang® Grid paper.

Erwin Indrawan

STEP 2 - Line out a grid on the chalkboard using a yard/meter stick. The large grid should be proportional to paper sketch grid.

STEP 3 - Transfer the design by scaling up the artwork using the grid method.

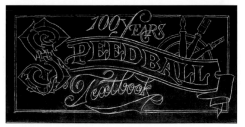

STEP 4 - Erase the grid lines and add details to complete your design.

The basic principles for what we now call "layout and design" are found throughout history. Before the graphic design processes of paste-up and photo reproduction, these concepts were used for centuries by artists as they composed paintings and pictures. The division of spatial elements and using emphasis to create effects are all principles that must be understood for effective artwork.

The writings of early 20th century commercial artists like Ross F. George are detailed but concise explanations of these principles, and he was continually refining these explanations from edition to edition.

The text and illustrations in the following pages come from the Speedball Textbook, 11th Edition (1929) and beginning and experienced artists alike will find these pages full of design wisdom.

> *"Even good lettering, correctly spaced, is ineffective if poorly arranged."*
> **Ross F. George**

SCALING PROPORTIONATELY

Enlarging and reducing an image by hand is done by making sure the original is the same proportion as the desired size. By extending diagonal lines through the drawing, any point may be readily located to replicate at the new size.
See page 101 for using the grid method of scaling.

BALANCING THE LAYOUT

Excerpted from The Speedball Textbook, 11th Edition (1929)
Ross F. George

"Layout" is the printing industry's term for the arrangement of "copy." It is a very important subject for even good lettering, correctly spaced, is ineffective if poorly arranged. Copy containing only a few words, and perhaps an illustration, is not hard to layout. But copy consisting of many phrases, sentences, paragraphs and illustrations can be better handled when it has been carefully divided into appropriate blocks before any attempt is made to arrange it on the card.

The quickest way to learn how to balance a layout is to treat all words, illustrations, border ornaments and color masses as though they were children's building blocks. Group the word blocks into larger phrase blocks (though sometimes a single word is a block

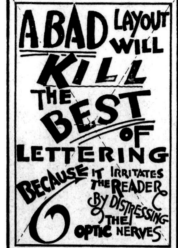

in itself), and then balance all pictures, spots of color or decorative masses with these phrase blocks according to their size and attraction. It is easy to see how this scheme minimizes layout problems

because, instead of a lot of individual words, there are only a few masses or groups to fit into a given space. By keeping the blocks simple in shape it is not difficult to arrange them in a pleasing and effective manner. By making a dummy layout on paper and cutting out the different blocks you can shift them around until you are satisfied with the layout before applying the ink.

When there is considerable copy to go on a card it should not all be done in the same size lettering. This would make the poster look like a page out of a book. The difference in the size of the lettering naturally depends upon the relative importance of the various words or phrase blocks.

Bottom-Heavy Layout

Pleasingly Balanced

Bad Layout - Poor arrangement distresses the optical nerves.

Better Layout - Groups or blocks are balanced upon optical center.

The arrangement and balance of unrelated masses and the apportioning of harmonious margins. Ross F. George, The Speedball Textbook, 11th Edition (1929).

OPTICAL CENTER LAYOUT

Excerpted from Speedball Textbook 11th Edition (1929)

Layouts which are perfectly balanced upon true center, with equal margins all around, will appear bottom heavy. This is just another of the many tricks our eyes play on us. Artists or letterers with a good sense of balance make an instinctive effort to counteract this by placing the copy higher on the card, about five percent above the actual center. Since this point is usually measured by the eye, it is called the "optical center."

Allow a thirty percent wider margin at the bottom than at the top with proportions something like this: 4 for the sides, 5 for the top and 7 for the bottom. This serves as a safe working guide which, of course, may be varied as conditions demand.

For those who find layouts difficult to arrange, the examples in this book should prove helpful. In balancing a block of copy with an illustration, color mass, or price, the center of attraction in each determines their positions on the poster (see page 103). When the attraction is equal, they are balanced at like distances from the optical center. Should one have greater attraction than another, it is balanced proportionately nearer to the optical center.

Another good method of determining when the poster is balanced is to pin it up on the wall and with half-closed eyes study the arrangement of the various blocks or masses. When it seems to hang with an equal division of the values on either side, you may be pretty sure that the layout is all right.

Many of the difficulties encountered by beginners are caused by trying to get too much big copy on a card. The purpose of a show card or poster is to attract attention, make an announcement or sell something and the copy should be limited, if possible, to the essential information. When too much copy is supplied without authority to cut it, play up the feature points for the main and subordinate headings then subdue the rest of the copy so as not to detract from these.

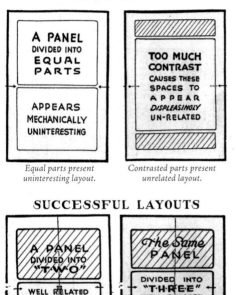

Balanced layouts place copy higher than midpoint with margins all around shown above.

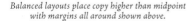

106

XTREME 1

Legacies 2

With
Pen
in Hand
THE JOURNEY of
AMERICAN HANDWRITING   3

Zen
GARDEN 4

Frankenstein 5

Marie Callender's 6

Indianapolis
IAMPETH 2014   7

1. John Burns 2. Martin Jackson 3. John Stevens 4. John Burns 5. Carl Rohrs 6. John Stevens 7. Don Marsh

Pasta 1

Grandfather 2

Luxe Paperie 3

Barefoot **WINERY** 5

Castles 4

Society for Calligraphy 6

Bonello 7

Harvest Selections 8

Calligraphy 9

1. John Burns 2. Charles Borges de Oliveira 3. Jill Bell 4. Rick Cusick 5. Jill Bell
6. Lisa Engelbrecht 7. John Burns 8. Charles Borges de Oliveira 9. Carl Rohrs

Erwin Indrawan

Larry Brady

Heather Held

Yukimi Annand

FAIRY TALES

Yukimi Annand

Janet Takahashi

Yves Letterme

Louie Lemoine

CONTEMPORARY LETTERING

Cinque sono gli elementi del libro, **Testo,**
Carattere, Inchiostro,
Carta &

Comporre con questi cinque elementi   per quanto può ester dato a opere fatte da uomini,
un tutto coerente e plausibile,   dagli influssi del capriccio e del caso,
non sottoposto alla moda,   e degne dell'alto retaggio di cui siamo
il cui pregio sia stabile e sciolto dal tempo;   depositari e responsabili :
comporne delle opere affrancate,   questa è la nostra ambizione.

Legatura.

GIOVANNI
MARDERSTEIG
CREDO · 1929

Luca Barcellona

John Stevens

CONTEMPORARY LETTERING

Have no fear
of perfection
You'll never
reach it.

SALVADOR DALÍ

Luca Barcellona

Weaving the
American
Dream

Don Marsh

Gothic Splendor

Barry Morentz

CONTEMPORARY LETTERING

Enamel on blown glass, Leslie Tardy

Hand-carved, gilded and painted on slate, Paul Herrera

Brush marker on stone, Linda Schneider

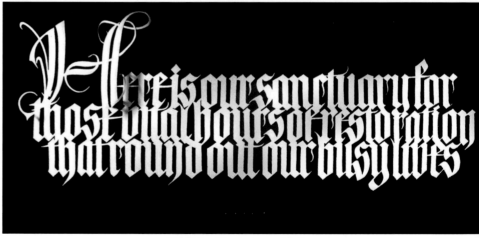

Hand-lettered, hand-cut paper, Julie Gray

CONTEMPORARY LETTERING

LOVE
Bears all things
Believes all things
Hopes all things
Endures all things

I CORINTHIANS 3:7

Ink, gouache and gilding, Cliff Mansley

The Night is long and
I am pondering for a peace
in my heart clean and
pure undisturbed

in the days that follow
the silent and still
breath and light

AND BE STILL AND KNOW THERE IS LOVE

Sharon Zeugin

Children of some future age
Reading this indignant page
Know that in a former time
Love, sweet love was thought a crime.

William Blake

Reggie Ezell

Contemporary Versals with a C-6 nib, Angela Vangalis
Quote by Reginald Vincent Holmes

Hand-lettered, hand-cut paper and fabric, Carl Rohrs

Inked to mimic woodcut, Robert Saslow

Modified Neuland with patterned drawing, CC Sadler

Decorated and Illuminated letters
1. Sharon Hanse 2. Risa Gettler 3. Harvest Crittenden 4. Barbara Close 5. Vivian Mungall 6. Joanne Fink 7. Judy Detrick 8. Janet Takahashi

 KNOTTED ETTERS

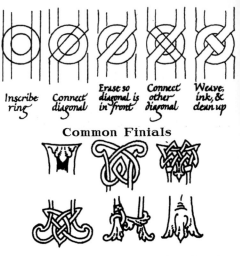

1. Sketch outlines of UNCIALESQUE or LOMBARDIC' versal letters.

2. Split them: Draw them as if constructed from narrow ribbons of metal. Note the ribbons' width remains constant.

3. Add fleur-de-lys finials to the letter terminals.

4. Entwine 'lifesaver' knot in the widest parts of each letter, & color internal spaces.

Mark Van Stone

Knotted Letters are *Versals* combined with *Celtic Knotwork*.

A *Knotted Letter* with brightly colored internal spaces can be used as a decorative capital.

The most abundant style of *Medieval Versal* decoration is *filigree pen work*. Usually done in contrasting colors, the first step is to outline the initial and a box to contain the decoration with fine double outlines. Fill the spaces with a trio of tiny concave triangles. Fill the triangles with tiny white leaves and vines.

Filigree Pen Work

Decorative Initials by Ross F. George and borders by William Hugh Gordon, The Speedball Textbook, 17th and 2nd Editions (1956) (1916).

GLOSSARY

Ascender - The part of the stroke in minuscule letters which extends above the waistline as in "b," "d," "f," "h," "k" and "l." The t has an abbreviated ascender.

Ascender line - The guideline showing the height of an ascending letter.

Base line - The line on which the letters rest.

Branching - The method by which the second stroke of a letter exits or joins to the stem stroke.

Broad-edge - A calligraphic term for flat-edged pen lettering to create a thick and thin line variation according to the angle of the pen. Pen nibs for this type of calligraphic mark include the Speedball A-Series, B-Series, C-Series and Steel Brush.

Built-up - A letter that is carefully drawn instead of written, then filled in with ink, patterning or gilding.

Capital line - Also referred to as "Cap Height" or "Cap line." The guideline showing the height of a capital letter.

Counter - Fully or partially enclosed space within a letter.

Cover sheet - A piece of paper that protects artwork from hand oils.

Cross bar - Horizontal stroke forming part of a letter (as in the letters "t," "A" and "H.")

Descender - The part of the minuscule letter which extends below the base line (as in "f," "g," "j," "p," "q," "y" and sometimes "z").

Descender line - The guideline showing the lowest part of a letter below the base line.

Down stroke - A stroke directed downwards toward the base line or descender line.

Ductus - Latin for "leading." The directional instruction for making the strokes of letters.

Entry stroke - The beginning of a stroke that leads into the letter itself.

Exemplar - Shows the characteristics of each letter in an alphabet style.

Exit stroke - The method of ending the last stroke of a letter, sometimes used to join to the next letter as in *Italic.*

Filament - A slender threadlike fiber, especially one found in animal or plant structures used for making brushes.

Flange - The protruding part that holds the nib in an oblique pen holder.

Flourish - An ornamental flowing curve in calligraphy or scroll-work.

Flourishing zone - The area above the ascender and below the descender line.

Font - A set of type of one particular face and size.

Gilding - The process of applying gold leaf or gold paint. Other metals such as palladium, copper or silver can also be used.

Glyph - In typography, an elemental symbol within an agreed set of symbols, intended to represent a readable character for the purposes of writing and thereby expressing thoughts, ideas and concepts.

Gothic - In calligraphic letter styles, *Gothic* refers to the historical hands which began in the late 11th century. Written with a broad-edged tool, they include *Blackletter* and *Textura,* along with the hands that are derived from *Blackletter* and *Textura,* including: *Bastarda;*

Gothicized Italic; Rotunda; and *Fraktur.* In the printing industry and for commercial lettering, *Gothic* refers to an alphabet with characters composed of strokes of uniform line width. These written characters are the reason that the first Speedball nibs were invented.

Gouache - Opaque watercolor with a solid white pigment such as chalk (or sometimes acrylic) added for opacity.

Gum Arabic - A water-soluble gum obtained from several leguminous plants of the genus Acacia used in the food industry and in glue, as the binder for watercolor paints.

Hand - A calligraphic style of lettering.

Hairlines - Thin, fine strokes usually made with a light touch by using the corner of a broad-edged pen or very light upward strokes of a pointed pen.

Illumination - A decorated, capital letter or illustration embellished with metal leaf, usually gold.

Ink stick - A type of solid ink used traditionally in several East Asian cultures for calligraphy and brush painting. Stick ink must be ground on a stone with drops of water to make ink.

Inter-letter space - The space between letters which is adjusted or *kerned* for better readability.

Interlinear space - The space between lines of text which is adjusted to suit the alphabet style. See *leading.*

Inter-word space - The space between words which is adjusted or *kerned* to fit within a line of text.

Italic - Any lettering that is forward slanted but not necessarily compressed. Also refers to the printing industry used synonymously with type and font terminology.

Kern - To adjust the spacing between letters (or characters) to make them more appealing.

Kerning pair - Commonly kerned pairs of letters with the spacing already adjusted for best visual appearance so that manual kerning is unnecessary.

Knotwork. - Ornamental work consisting of or representing intertwined and knotted cords.

Leading - A term used to measure the vertical space between lines from base line to base line of text. See Inter-linear space

Letterform - The graphic form of a letter of the alphabet, either as written or in a particular type font.

Ligature - Two or more letters are joined together to form one character written by hand or digitally in a typeface glyph.

Majuscule - A capital or uppercase letter.

Manipulation - Turning the pen and/or hand at different angles to create varied marks.

Mahlstick - A light-weight stick with a padded leather or rubber ball at one end, held against work by a painter or sign writer to support and steady the brush hand.

Minuscule - A lowercase letter.

Nib - The part of a dip pen, fountain pen or quill used with a writing fluid. Available in a variety of points, shapes and sizes in two categories: *Broad-edged* and *Pointed*.

Nib width - The unit of measurement of any broad-edged tool used to determine the proportion of a letter form.

Oblique holder - A pen staff that holds a pointed pen nib at an offset angle designed for better angle/slant while writing and attaining an even distribution of pressure.

Pangram - A sentence that contains every letter of the alphabet. Also called an Abecedarian sentence. Waltz, nymph, for quick jigs vex Bud. Sphinx of black quartz, judge my vow.

Pen angle - The angle of the nib in relation to the base line of the lettering line. Many calligraphy styles have the pen pointed roughly perpendicular to the upper left hand corner of the page at various degrees.

Pen point - See *Nib*.

Pen wipe - A small piece of chamois leather, dampened and used for wiping excess ink off a pen nib. This piece of chamois can also aid in fitting a nib into a pen holder without damaging the nib while protecting the fingers from sharp pointed nibs.

Pointed pen - A nib with a sharp point used primarily for pressure and release writing.

Pressure - Applying strokes with gradual exertion and finally releasing with the lightest touch using a metal nib, brush or pencil to define the line quality.

Reservoir - An additional piece of metal added to the nib to create a capillary action for ink flow and to hold more ink or paint.

Roman - Alphabets written with a broad-edged tool that are generally upright.

Sans serif - Without serif or "feet." Derived from the French word for "without."

Serifs - Non-structural details at the beginning and endings of a stroke. There are various types of serifs including bracketed, full and half slab, and double bracketed.

Shade - The thick lines created on down strokes by pushing down on a pointed pen nib with an even motion.

Shoe - The flat part of the bottom of the Speedball A-, B-, or D-Series nibs that rest on the marking surface in order to make a mark which is the shape of the nib.

Slant - The sloping position of calligraphy or handwriting used as a guide for writing against.

Spacing
 Counter space - The space inside a letter.
 Inter-letter space - The space between letters
 Interlinear space - The space between lines of writing.
 Inter-word space - The space between words.

Stem stroke - The primary, upright stroke that forms the structure of a letter.

Stick ink - See *Ink stick*.

Typeface - Represents one aspect of a font. There are two general categories of typefaces, serif and sans serif.

Waisting - A tapered line of intentionally varied thickness (vs. a straight line of equal thickness) used in *Versals* and pressurized letterforms.

Waist line - The top line of the x-height of a letter, as measured in pen widths from the base line.

X-height - The height of the body of a minuscule or lowercase letter, measured in pen nib widths from the base line.

INDEX

REFERENCES

Foundations of Calligraphy by Sheila Waters. 126 pages; John Neal Bookseller, (2006) ISBN: 0-9665305-1-9.

Writing and Illuminating and Lettering by Edward Johnston. 480 pages; Dover Publications (1995), ISBN: 978-0486285344

Write Now: The Getty Dubay Program for Handwriting Success by Getty Dubay. 96 pages; Fahrney's Exclusive; 3rd edition (2011) ISBN-13: 978-0982776223.

COLOPHON

Most of the typefaces used throughout this book were inspired by lettering produced by William Hugh Gordon in The Speedball Textbook, 2nd Edition (1916).

Adobe® Jenson Pro body copy by Robert Slimbach (based on Type Designer, Nicolas Jenson - 15th century). William Hugh Gordon published his attempt to mimic Jenson's work (see below).

LHF ROSS ANTIQUE ROMAN Section headings by John Studden inspired by Gordon's Alphabet first appearing in The Speedball Textbook, 2nd Edition (1916).

Speedball Ragged by Intellecta Design based on Western Letters by Ross F. George, 7th Edition (1923).

Jensen Bold Condensed
abcdefghijklmnopqrstuvwxyz
ABCDEFGHIJKLMNOPQRSTUVWXYZ

ABCDEFGHIJKLM
NOPQRSTUVWXYZ
abcdefghijklmnop
qrstuvwwxyz &

William Hugh Gordon
The Speedball Textbook, 2nd Edition (1916)